YOUR
SPIRITUAL BIRTHDAY

PRESENTED TO

_____

FROM

_____

DATE

_____

NOTE

_____

_____

_____

_____

YOUR SPIRITUAL BIRTHDAY

REJOICE AND CELEBRATE

JAMES B. SIEBKEN

Foreword By
MARK MITTELBERG

EQUIP PRESS

Colorado Springs

YOUR SPIRITUAL BIRTHDAY

First Edition 2019
Your Spiritual Birthday: Rejoice and Celebrate
Paperback: 978-1-946453-83-9
eBook: 978-1-946453-84-6

EQUIP PRESS

Colorado Springs

DEDICATION

I dedicate this book to Brianna, Zachary, Foster, Sullivan, Eliza, Nolan, Peyton, Kennedy, Daria, Alexanna, and Quincy, my eleven grandchildren. Their SPIRITUAL BIRTHDAYS are my inspiration for writing this book. May we rejoice and celebrate together forever.

contents

FOREWORD

"Praise be to the God and Father of our Lord Jesus Christ!" enthused the Apostle Peter in 1 Peter 1:3. What made Peter feel so exuberant and full of worship? He tells us in the verses that follow.

"In his great mercy *he has given us new birth* into a living hope through the resurrection of Jesus Christ from the dead, and *into an inheritance that can never perish, spoil or fade.* This inheritance is *kept in heaven for you* who through faith are shielded by God's power..." (1 Peter 1:3-5, emphases mine).

In effect, Peter was summoning all of us who have trusted in Christ, grabbing our shoulders and shaking us, and telling us to wake up and get excited because we have been given a new spiritual birth by God himself. We therefore have much to rejoice about, to celebrate, and to share with others.

The author of this book, J. B. Siebken, is also enthralled by the realization that through Christ we have a new birth, and he is adamant that we need to therefore remember our spiritual birthday each year in a heartfelt celebration. As you read these pages, I'm confident you'll catch his contagious enthusiasm in ways that will mark you and impact others through you.

Now, full disclosure: The author is a man I've known all my life as "Uncle Jim." In fact, I've even been guilty of calling him my *favorite* uncle—but please don't mention that to my other uncles!

Why have I always been so enthusiastic about Jim? There are many reasons, including the fact that he was always so kind and encouraging to me as I was growing up. In addition, he has always been quite impressive. He's a veritable math whiz, a world-class engineer, a successful businessman—even serving a high-end engineering and construction firm for many years as its President and CEO, and he's an effective church leader who knows how to rally support and get things done.

But more than these public attributes, I've always been impressed by Jim's gentle, generous spirit and godly, Christlike example. And as you're about to discover for yourself, Jim loves God deeply and cares about people passionately—and he wants to do everything he can to introduce them to each other.

All these elements combine to make me proud to introduce you to James B. Siebken—one of the most wonderful people I know.

Jim has an uncanny awareness of the eternal. For years he has printed up plaques and T-shirts to give to friends and family with inscriptions about heaven, reminding us that there's nothing more important than doing whatever it takes to be sure we'll someday *Be There*. His other incessant theme is the main subject of this book: that we need to make sure we've genuinely had an initial spiritual birthday, that we do our best to figure out when it was (or pick a date, as he'll discuss), and then that we celebrate it regularly as a way to honor God and proclaim his goodness to others.

This is Jim's book, so I don't want to steal any more of his thunder. Let me just add one last thought: There is no topic on earth, no theme explored, and no subject written about that is more important than the central idea of what's in the pages ahead. Jim is right: nothing matters more than understanding God's plan of salvation, putting our faith in Christ in order to make sure we'll end up one day in heaven with him, and proclaiming his truth to the people around us so that they, too, can know him now and into eternity.

I hope you'll read this book with an open heart, and I trust you'll heed its message with an enthusiastic spirit.

Oh, and may I be among the first to wish you a Happy Spiritual Birthday?

> *I will remember the deeds of the Lord;*
> *yes, I will remember your miracles of long ago.*
> *I will consider all your works*
> *and meditate on all your mighty deeds.*
> **- Psalm 77:11-12**

MARK MITTELBERG

Bestselling author of *The Questions Christians Hope No One Will Ask (With Answers)*, *Confident Faith*, and the *Becoming a Contagious Christian* training course.

introduction

Iesus was very clear when he spoke of the need for your spiritual birthday. *Very truly, I tell you, no one can see the kingdom of God without being born again* (John 3:3). He clarified and reinforced your need:

> *Very truly, I tell you, no one can enter the kingdom of God*
> *without being born of water and the Spirit. Flesh gives birth*
> *to flesh, but the Spirit gives birth to spirit. You should not be*
> *surprised at my saying, "You must be born again."*
>
> **(John 3:5-7)**

The Apostle John makes it clear that Jesus is speaking not only to Nicodemus, a Jewish religious leader, but is speaking to all born of flesh. If we believe that John 3:16, *"For God so loved the world that he gave his one and only Son, that whoever believes in him shall not perish but have eternal life."* includes us, we also must believe that *"You must be born again."* includes us.

You must be physically born of your mother to see and enter the world. You must be spiritually born of the Spirit to see and enter the kingdom of God. Your physical birth is recorded by the government, celebrated by your parents, and establishes your citizenship on earth. Your spiritual birth is recorded by Jesus in his Book of Life, celebrated by angels of God in heaven, and establishes your citizenship in heaven.

Christians around the world annually celebrate their physical birthdays, but few celebrate their spiritual birthdays. It is time for Christians to rejoice and celebrate their spiritual birthdays annually as a testimony of God's amazing grace and the joy of being an eternal child of God. It is difficult to imagine not celebrating this life-changing event. In Jesus' Parable of the Prodigal Son, the father told the older brother, *But we had to celebrate and be glad, because this brother of yours was dead, and is alive again; he was lost, and is found* (Luke 15:32).

Christian churches celebrate Christ's physical birthday on December 25, and his death and resurrection on Easter. Many churches celebrate Pentecost Sunday when the Holy Spirit came as Jesus promised. Pentecost Sunday resulted in three thousand spiritual birthdays. The Christian church needs to celebrate spiritual birthdays as the reason for and result of these three events.

The focus of this book is on you rejoicing and celebrating your spiritual birthday. May your celebrating be contagious as you share your joy with family, friends, and your church.

CHAPTER 1

YOUR
PHYSICAL BIRTHDAY

As you do not know the path of the wind,
Or how the body is formed in a mother's womb,
So you cannot understand the work of God,
The Maker of all things.

(Ecclesiastes 11:5)

Have you ever tried to imagine your physical birthday? Can you imagine the emotions and drama on the day you were physically born? You were there in the starring role, but you do not remember your performance. Can you imagine the day and the supporting cast? Today, some parents video the physical birth of their child to preserve this big event and replay it for family or later show it to their child. But a video might not be as big of an attraction as they believed. Some things might be better left to your imagination or to your Mother's memories! Photographs of newborn babies cleaned up and wrapped in pink or blue soft blankets have always been popular with parents and grandparents to show to all their friends and anyone they meet. You likely have seen your baby picture but do not carry it now to show others.

If you are a parent, you can better imagine your day of birth and all the pride and excitement. Your arrival was likely met with rejoicing and celebration by your parents, family, and friends. As a parent of three children and grandparent of nine, I have rejoiced and celebrated each birthday with excitement and pride. Every physical birth is a mysterious and miraculous event that never ceases to amaze and bless parents. Yours was no exception.

YOUR PHYSICAL BIRTHDAY IS IMPORTANT

There are no exceptions when it comes to physical births; you must be born to enter this physical world. All 7.5 billion+ human citizens have been physically born and have a physical birthday. On average, it means that over twenty million people share your physical birthday (month and day). Yet your physical birthday is very important to you, and I imagine you continue to celebrate it each year. Your physical birth is also important to the government, which records your vital statistics on your birth certificate and keeps it on file. Your birth certificate certifies that you were born alive at a specific time and date but contains very little else about your physical birthday. Do you know your birth weight and length? This information is usually provided to parents by the attending nurses and recorded in your birth announcements and baby book. Baby books record your early years, according to your mother, and are great to read and share in your older years. Hopefully, your mother filled out a baby book for you.

YOUR BIRTH STORY

You know the Who, What, When, and Where of your birth story, but do you know the Why and How of your birth story? The Why is not recorded on your birth certificate and may not have been shared by your mother in your baby book. You may have even asked yourself during discouraging times, "Why was I even born?" Some people want to blame God, but Scripture says that you were physically born by natural descent because of the human desire and will of your biological parents. God created the first man and woman, blessed them, and said to them, *Be fruitful and increase in number, fill the earth and subdue it* (Genesis 1:28). God's plan and blessing to mankind to fill the earth was given with their choice to multiply through natural descent. Except for Jesus, who was born of a virgin, all physical births have been through natural descent by two biological parents. God's plan is for a woman to have a choice, but it does not include the right of a woman to change her mind once a child is conceived. Thankfully, your mother made the right choice, and that is why you were physically born.

IT IS IN YOUR DNA

The answer to How you were physically born is much more miraculous and mysterious than the five W questions. You now realize that the pictures or stories of a long-legged stork delivering you suspended in a blanket were fiction. You understand that the Why decision was made months before your physical birthday. How much do you know or even imagine about your physical life before your physical birth? Scientists and physicians have studied and learned much about the physical development of a human being between conception and birth, but much of the How remains a mystery or at best a theory. A rather recent (1953) discovery by scientists is deoxyribonucleic acid, better known as DNA. It was not until 2001 that the true nature and complexity of the digital code inherent in DNA was known. The genetics molecule establishes every living organism's physical characteristics. This code is contained in every cell of every organism and contains specific and unique information regarding genetic and physical characteristics. The details and workings of DNA are too complex for me to imagine, let alone comprehend and explain here. If you desire to learn more specific scientific details of DNA and the human genome, Wikipedia and The Human Genome Project are good resources.

As a civil engineer by profession, I am interested in how things are created. Engineers create physical machines and structures from non-living materials. We develop detailed plans and specifications on how the materials and parts are to be combined to create the machine or structure.

I am going to give you my simplified engineering analysis on how you were physically created. I believe that DNA is God's creation mechanism for human beings and all other living organisms. Since your unique DNA code contains information regarding your parents and their ancestral lineage, God did not begin to create your physical form until your biological parents made their decision to conceive a child. God's plan for reproduction requires equal input by mother and father. Each normal human cell has twenty-three chromosome pairs (forty-six total) and one DNA molecule. During human sexual reproduction, normal cells divide, forming special cells—sperm in males and eggs in females, which have twenty-three single chromosomes. During the fertilization stage, a special cell from each parent merges into one embryo with twenty-three pairs of chromosomes (twenty-three from your mother and twenty-three from your father) forming your unique DNA molecule.

Your physical body is formed as cells, each reflecting your human species and your genetics inherited from each parent, divided and built according to the instructions contained in your DNA or, as I like to think of it, as God's plans and specifications. DNA determines which cells become bone or flesh or hair or an eye and so on. Some cells are formed in the womb, some in childhood, others later during puberty and even later as we age. When your body is to stop producing growth cells or start forming healing cells is contained in your DNA. Each cell continues to carry the complete DNA sequencing code or number as they are formed. I have seen the detailed plans and specification required to build large specialized buildings, including hospitals and water treatment plants, but none compare to the detail of your DNA instruction to not only build but to also maintain your physical body. Actually, less than 1 percent of your DNA instructions are unique to you when compared to all human DNA. The difference between your DNA and other living species is much greater.

YOUR LIFE BEFORE BIRTH

Can you imagine your life after conception and before you were born? Your mother probably did not record or tell you much about your conception. The subject is generally too personal to share with others. You may have seen ultrasound photos of yourself or your own child in the womb. Ultrasounds are usually not very clear to the untrained eye and do require your imagination. Your prenatal development is best illustrated in books and on websites. If you imagine that the photos, illustrations, and descriptions of the fetus at each week or month are of you, it makes your development more personal and amazing.

You and your mother had a very close relationship during your prenatal development. She supplied your physical needs to survive and grow in a very warm, dark, and liquid environment. Your heart started beating by the eighth week after conception, but you were on life support from Mom. You were soon moving and kicking her to show your appreciation. Fetus growth slows after week thirty-six and full-term is considered thirty-nine or forty weeks. Your unique physical features develop in the last weeks of your birth-line. The average full-term newborn is about twenty inches long, which is more than 25 percent of their adult height. Your head was more than half of your length and your legs were very short. Fortunately for your mother, your skull had movable plates that allowed it to elongate during birth.

Your birth was initiated when your mother's physical body determined that you were ready to leave the security of your dark and fluid environment to launch out on your own. It was a big change as you took your first breath of air with your untried lungs. People were holding your body in new positions and trying to dry you off. Your mother was happy, but all you could do was cry.

SURVIVING YOUR BIRTH DAY

Fortunately, you were born with a survival instinct, and your physical body knew how to respond to your new environment. Your heart was beating fast on its own and your mouth was ready to find nourishment from your mother in a new way. With help from her and the attending hospital staff, you survived the single most dangerous day of your life. More humans die on their birthday than any other day. According to a study by *Save The Children* in 2013, a million babies die every year globally on the day they are born. The report estimates that 11,300 American newborns die on their birthday each year, which is a higher rate than any other industrialized country.

On a personal note, I have a younger brother who survived his birthday and is still living at age seventy-seven. However, I have a brother, twin brothers, and a sister who did not survive their physical birthday. My mother's DNA and father's DNA caused their blood to have different Rh factors, which caused Rh disease in these babies. Rh disease was a serious health concern in the middle of the twentieth century, causing death to 10,000 babies in the U.S. every year. Thankfully, a vaccine approved in 1968 has eliminated the threat of Rh blood disease to newborns.

You not only survived your physical birthday but many more days and years. You have grown in stature physically and in the knowledge of your physical world. May you survive and enjoy many more years on planet earth. As you celebrate your birthday, the anniversary of your physical birth, remember the why and how of your birth, as well as the years of your physical life. Your amazing birth is a good reason to rejoice and celebrate each and every physical birthday.

CHAPTER 2

YOUR
SPIRITUAL BIRTHDAY

You should not be surprised at my saying,
"You must be born again."
(John 3:7)

Can you imagine that, according to Genesis 1:27, you were created in the image and likeness of God? Do you imagine the image of God to be a physical body or a spiritual being? The attributes of God described in Scripture are spiritual rather than physical. The visible image of your physical body that you see in a mirror confirms that you are a physical being with a physical birthday. Your physical image shows your shape, size, color, and age, but there is much more to know about you than your physical body. The mirror or photographs of you do not reveal your personality, your intellect, your values, your feelings, or your dreams. Your non-physical nature or soul reveals who you really are as a human being. Our human spirit is what distinguishes us from all other living creatures. Human

23

beings were created in the spiritual image of God. Your spiritual image is not visible in a mirror, but God's image and likeness is revealed in the Bible.

How you imagine God will depend on how you understand the Bible. Do you imagine the Bible as the inspired word of God, which reveals his attributes and nature? One of the descriptions of God that may be difficult to grasp is that of the Trinity: one God in three persons—Father, Son, and Holy Spirit. One of the most quoted verses in Scripture is John 3:16, *For God so loved the world that he gave his one and only Son, that whoever believes in him shall not perish but have eternal life.* John 1:18 says; *No one has ever seen God, but the one and only Son, who himself is God and is in closest relationship with the Father, has made him known.* Jesus testified about God the Father in John 4:24; *God is spirit, and his worshipers must worship in the Spirit and in truth.*

How you imagine Jesus the Son may be more important than how you imagine God the Father. Jesus is referred to in Scripture as the Son of God and as the Son of Man. He was spiritually the son of God the Father, and physically the son of Mary. He was both divine and human in nature. Several religions, including Judaism and Islam, believe in one God but do not believe that Jesus is God the Son. It is hard for me to imagine that the evidence of Jesus' divinity, through early manuscripts by eyewitnesses to his life, resurrection, and fulfilled prophecy, can be denied. They have been studied and challenged for centuries and have been proven true.

You need to understand that the Bible is the trustworthy source of spiritual truth about God and his relationship with human beings. I will refer to specific passages from the Bible throughout this book, assuming that you have access to a Bible and a basic understanding of Scripture. I encourage you to read God's book for spiritual truth, and I hope this book, *Your Spiritual Birthday*, will be an incentive to study it more.

YOU MUST BE BORN AGAIN

Can you imagine being "born again" or having a "spiritual birth"? These terms are not words coined by me or by a church but by Jesus, to explain eternal life to a Jewish leader. Jesus' encounter with Nicodemus is recorded in John 3:1-21.

> Now there was a Pharisee, a man named Nicodemus, who was a member of the Jewish ruling council. He came to Jesus at night and said, "Rabbi, we know that you are a teacher who has come from God. For no one could perform the signs you are doing if God were not with him."

> Jesus replied, "Very truly I tell you, no one can see the kingdom of God unless they are born again."

> "How can someone be born when they are old?" Nicodemus asked. "Surely they cannot enter a second time into their mother's womb to be born."

Jesus answered, "Very truly I tell you, no one can enter the kingdom of God unless they are born of water and the Spirit. Flesh gives birth to flesh, but the Spirit gives birth to spirit. You should not be surprised at my saying, 'You must be born again.' The wind blows wherever it pleases. You hear its sound, but you cannot tell where it comes from or where it is going. So it is with everyone born of the Spirit."

"How can this be?'" Nicodemus asked.

"You are Israel's teacher," said Jesus, "and do you not understand these things? Very truly I tell you, we speak of what we know, and testify to what we have seen, but still you people do not accept our testimony. I have spoken to you of earthly things and you do not believe; how then will you believe if I speak of heavenly things? No one has ever gone into heaven except the one who came from heaven—the Son of Man. Just as Moses lifted up the snake in the wilderness, so the Son of Man must be lifted up, that everyone who believes may have eternal life in him.

"For God so loved the world that he gave his one and only Son, that whoever believes in him shall not perish but have eternal life. For God did not send his Son into the world to condemn the world, but to save the world through him.

Whoever believes in him is not condemned, but whoever does not believe stands condemned already because they have not believed in the name of God's one and only Son. This is the verdict: Light has come into the world, but people loved darkness instead of light because their deeds were evil. All those who do evil hate the light, and will not come into the light for fear that their deeds will be exposed. But those who live by the truth come into the light, so that it may be seen plainly that what they have done has been done in the sight of God."

John 3 is a very important, if not the most important, chapter in Scripture. It includes John 3:16, which is recognized by many Bible scholars as the most famous summary of the gospel in the entire Bible. Bible scholars cannot agree on whether Verse 16 is Jesus still speaking to Nicodemus or is Apostle John commenting. There are no quotation marks in Greek manuscripts, so translators debate where Jesus' speech ends and John's commentary begins. Some translations have verses 16–21 in red type, indicating Jesus speaking, and other translations have those verses in black type, indicating John is speaking as inspired by the Holy Spirit.

I encourage you to read it through several times and in several translations, and to take the time to understand it thoroughly. I do not believe whether Jesus said or John wrote verses 16-21 changes the importance and truth of the teaching. The verses certainly tie well to verse 15 and to

Nicodemus coming to Jesus by night rather than in light. This teaching is clearly from Jesus himself and is the origin for the term "born-again" Christian. It is also the basis for *Your Spiritual Birthday*.

NICODEMUS MEETING WITH JESUS

The story has many important details. Who was Nicodemus? He was a Pharisee. The Pharisees were the Jewish interpreters and teachers of the Mosaic Law in synagogues during the time of Jesus. They were a legalistic group who strictly, but often hypocritically, tried to keep the Law of Moses and the unwritten "tradition of the elders." Nicodemus was also a member of the Jewish ruling council, or Sanhedrin, a smaller select group including Pharisees, chief priests, and elders. He was not just anyone; he was a high-ranking religious leader. Jesus knew who he was and called him one of Israel's teachers. Nicodemus came to Jesus at night. He came to where Jesus was staying under the cover of darkness, apparently because he didn't want the other religious leaders to know of his private visit. Jesus had taught in the Jewish synagogues and the public square, so Nicodemus had likely heard him.

Nicodemus opens the conversation by flattering, calling him "Rabbi." Pharisees loved to be called *Rabbi* by others. He continued, *We know that you are a teacher who has come from God. For no one could perform the signs you are doing if God were not with him.* He uses the plural "we," signifying that he is speaking for other Pharisees. Jesus knew the Pharisees continually denied that his teachings and signs came from God and that God was with him. His response directly related to a primary teaching of his ministry, the kingdom of God.

John the Baptist's early message was, *Repent, for the kingdom of heaven has come near* (Matthew 3:2). When Jesus began to preach, his message was, *Repent, for the kingdom of heaven has come near* (Matthew 4:17). Later, when villagers in Galilee begged Jesus not to leave them, he replied, *I must proclaim the good news of the kingdom of God to the other town also, because that is why I was sent* (Luke 4:43). The kingdom of God is mentioned over eighty times in the synoptic gospels of Matthew, Mark, and Luke. John only used the term twice in his gospel, quoting Jesus' discussion with Nicodemus.

Jesus made it very clear what is required to see and enter the kingdom of God. *Very truly I tell you, no one can see the kingdom of God unless they are born again.* "Very truly I tell you" emphasized it was trustworthy, and Jesus says it twice to indicate its importance. Jesus could be very strong in condemning Pharisees and their hypocrisy, yet here he was strong in his concern and counsel to Nicodemus regarding the kingdom of God. Nicodemus could not imagine being born again and asks Jesus how someone can be born when they are old. He was sure of the obvious impossibility that an adult cannot re-enter their mother's womb and be born physically a second time. Jesus again emphasizes and clarifies that no one can enter the kingdom of God unless they are born physically (of water). and spiritually (of the Spirit). Physical birth is by natural descent. Flesh gives birth to flesh. Spiritual birth is by the Holy Spirit.

The Spirit gives birth to spirit. Jesus thought Nicodemus should not be surprised by his saying, "You must be born again."

HOW CAN THIS BE?

He expected Nicodemus to understand the working of the Spirit from his studies of Moses and the Prophets, yet Nicodemus still questioned Jesus, *How can this be?* Do you also wonder "How can this be?" Can you imagine that you must be born again to see and to enter the kingdom of God? Do you believe that all Christians must be born-again Christians? Jesus challenged Nicodemus, asking, *You are Israel's teacher and you do not understand these things?*

Today, many of America's religious teachers, priests, and pastors do not understand these things. Some believe you are born again by water baptism, including infant baptism. Others consider spiritual birth a process and compare it to a physical pregnancy. Still others teach that you can be born again and again and again. Many even believe that being born again is not required for you to enter the kingdom of God.

Your physical birth occurred at a specific time and date once and was not a process. Your spiritual birthday is an event occurring at a specific time and date and not multiple times. It could be called your "Second Birthday," but "Spiritual Birthday" differentiates it from your physical birthday. You are physically born of your physical parents. You are spiritually born of God through the Spirit. You are physically born of water and spiritually born of Spirit. Flesh gives birth to flesh, but the Spirit gives birth to spirit. Physical birth is unto physical life and spiritual birth is unto eternal life. The result of these differences is summarized in the saying: "Born Once, Die Twice; Born Twice, Die Once."

SPIRITUAL BIRTH COMPARED TO PHYSICAL BIRTH

The process leading to your spiritual birth cannot be compared to a physical pregnancy. Your physical birth was expected and was probably not exceptional. Your parents had to follow God's standard plan for human reproduction to bring you into the world. Your mother gave physical birth to you, and you had no choice or involvement. However, God uses vastly differing circumstances and experiences to bring people to spiritual birth in Christ. C. H. Spurgeon, the famous English preacher, remarked, "God's Spirit calls men and women to Jesus in diverse ways. Some are drawn so gently that they scarcely know when the drawing began, and others are so suddenly affected that their conversion (spiritual birth) stands out with noonday clearness."

I recently heard a pastor, whose teachings I greatly respect, preach on being born again using 1 Peter 1:23 as his text. Peter, writing to Christians scattered throughout Asia Minor, reminded the believers of their spiritual birth, saying, *For you have been born again, not of perishable seed, but of imperishable, through the living and enduring word of God.* The pastor went on to explain that being born again is an event comparable to a wedding rather than a physical birth. As I listened to his love story of meeting, courting, and marrying his wife, I was reminded of my own love story of courting and marrying my wife.

MY LOVE STORY

I met Martie on a blind date in the fall of my second year of college. I had been dating a girl all through high school and my first year of college, but our colleges were sixty miles apart and distanced us from mutual friends and activities. A new acquaintance and chemistry lab partner, Roger, wanted me to go on a blind date with his girlfriend's sister, who had recently broken up with her boyfriend. We were to go to a local high school football game with him and her sister. After agreeing to go with them to the game, I began to have second thoughts about meeting a new girl. However, when I met her, I was glad I had not backed out. We had a nice evening together, even if my car would not start at the drive-in restaurant after the game.

It was not love at first sight, and I even told her that I would be continuing to see my old girlfriend (not too smart!). The following week, I had second thoughts and, with Roger's encouragement, found the courage to call her for a second date. I do not recall the evening except that my car would not start and I had to call my roommates for a battery boost, which they did with glee. Again, I told her that I would continue seeing my old girlfriend, and again I had second thoughts after a weekend at home.

On our third date, my car battery again failed, so I finally decided it was time to get a new battery along with the new girlfriend. As we dated, I knew I liked her and wanted to know more about her, her family, and her friends. The more I learned, the more I liked her, and I felt that maybe I was falling in love.

Eventually, I told Martie that I loved her. She told me that she loved me and, thankfully, I did not have any second thoughts. We spent more time together. I was a student and she was working for the state government, but she did not have a car so I would pick her up after work. We attended her church together, and I met several of her Christian friends and coworkers.

After a summer at home helping my father on the farm, and seeing her only on weekends, we realized we wanted to be together more. In the fall of my junior year, after asking her father for permission, I proposed to Martie and she said yes. Our engagement went by quickly as we planned our wedding and anticipated being together in marriage. Finally, after another summer of being miles apart, our August 29th wedding day arrived. We were married in her church, and I told her that I would attend church with her but would not become an active member.

As she walked down the aisle, I knew I was making the right decision to marry Martie. As I repeated the marriage vows, I realized that I was making a big commitment. I do not recall my exact words, but it was along the lines of: "I, James, take you, Martha, to be my wedded wife, to have and to hold from this day forward, for better or for worse, for richer or for poorer, in sickness and in health, to love and to cherish, till death us do part, according to God's holy ordinance. This is my solemn vow." I listened, with great emotion, as Martie repeated her vows. I think she even added "to obey" to the "to love and to cherish" part of her vow.

But we were still not married—not until the pastor proclaimed, "Now that Martha and James have given themselves to each other by solemn vows, with joining of hands and the giving and receiving of rings, I, in accordance with the powers granted me by the state, pronounce you husband and wife, in the Name of the Father, and of the Son, and of the Holy Spirit." At that pronouncement, we became a married couple. We became one flesh as Genesis 2:24 proclaims: *Therefore, a man shall leave his father and mother and hold fast to his wife, and they shall become one flesh.* A marriage certificate showing the date of our marriage was prepared, sealed, and recorded with the state as a legal record of this momentous event. The proclamation of marriage is comparable to the moment you are proclaimed spiritually born again by the Holy Spirit.

MY SPIRITUAL BIRTHDAY STORY

As I think about my love story and wedding, I compare them to my spiritual birthday story. My parents were members of a church that practiced infant baptism, so I was presented to the Lord when I was very young. They attended church infrequently, but when they did, I attended Sunday school classes and heard Bible stories about Jesus. At age twelve, I attended catechism classes, received instruction on Scripture, and memorized several doctrinal creeds. I was able to pass the final examination questions in front of the congregation and was confirmed as a member of the church. I viewed the confirmation by the church as more of an ending than a beginning. During my high school years, I did not attend church or youth activities. My parents did not practice prayer or Scripture reading in our home, so I had only limited head knowledge of spiritual truths and practices.

When I met Martie during my sophomore year in college, I soon discovered that she attended church regularly and that she had sung in a children's choir and a girl's trio on Back to the Bible's Saturday Radio Program for many years. She invited me to attend her church with her, and because I enjoyed being with her, I quickly agreed to these Sunday morning dates. But in the process, I learned much more about God, his Son Jesus, and the good news of the gospel. As I college student, I felt that I was gaining more knowledge about religion, but I was not feeling any emotion or need for action regarding the spiritual truths I heard preached. I imagined that I was already a member of a church and that I was not some kind of lost sinner.

Looking back, I imagined that I believed as Martie believed, and she imagined that I believed like she believed. Love can be blind. The Christian values and actions of Martie and her Christian family and friends were attractive to me. Their language, conduct, and faith during the week reflected the teachings I heard on Sunday mornings. After we were married, we attended her church, but I did not become active in church activities.

We had been married about nine months when I graduated from engineering college and took a job in California. Martie found secretarial work at the same large corporation, and we made new friends with our new co-workers. Being far from family and church friends, we found that the beach and other attractions filled our weekends, and we did not find a new church home. After about six months, our employer lost a large government contract and laid off many engineers, including me.

Thankfully, I quickly found engineering work with Los Angeles County, but it required me to travel in the opposite direction from where Martie worked. I soon found two county co-workers living near us and was able to arrange to ride with them. One, Warren Smith, was a born-again Christian. As we became friends, Warren invited Martie and me to go with him and his wife, Carlene, to the young married couples' class at their church. We were quickly drawn into the class by the teacher, who was very good, and by the other couples, who were very friendly. The class planned social and fellowship activities that we enjoyed and which helped us make new friends.

A few months after we started attending the class, the church held special meetings, with an evangelist speaking. I do not remember his message, but on that Thursday night, November 3, 1960, God, through the Holy Spirit, brought me to repentance and a personal saving faith in Christ. I publicly professed that I was a lost sinner and that my only hope for eternal life was through faith in Jesus. I asked Jesus to be my Lord and Savior and claimed his promises for a new life. I was born again and received the gift of the Holy Spirit. I did not repeat any vows or say, "I do," although to love and to cherish God from this day forward would have been appropriate. The "till death do us part" would not have been included since death will not part me from Jesus.

Martie recommitted her life to Christ that night, confessing that she was not living in accordance with his teachings. As a testimony to our faith in Jesus, we both were baptized by immersion to symbolize our passage from the old life into a new life with Christ.

EACH SPIRITUAL BIRTHDAY STORY UNIQUE

Your spiritual birthday story is unique. How and when you were introduced to Jesus will have a significant impact on your journey to faith. If your parents knew and loved the Lord and introduced you to him during your childhood, you may have been drawn to him as a young adult. If your parents did not know Jesus and used his name in vain, you may have not wanted, as an adult, to be introduced to him. The Holy Spirit is seeking the lost on behalf of Jesus and uses many people and circumstances to find you. Can you imagine the many spiritual birthday stories beginning with the three thousand who accepted Peter's message at Pentecost, repenting and believing in the name of Jesus Christ as their promised Savior? As they shared their spiritual birthday story with others, the Spirit added to their number daily those who were saved. The book of Acts, written by Luke, is referred to as the Acts of the Apostles but could also be considered the Acts of the Holy Spirit. A few early spiritual birthday stories like that of the Ethiopian eunuch, Paul, and Cornelius are recorded in Acts. Thousands more were added to the kingdom of God after hearing Paul's spiritual birthday story.

THE APOSTLE JOHN

John is the only gospel writer to record the meeting and conversation between Jesus and Nicodemus. You may wonder why the other three gospel writers mentioned the kingdom of God eighty times without explicitly tying it to being born again. John may have been the only apostle with Jesus on the night Nicodemus came to speak to Jesus. In reading Scripture, it is important to understand the writer and his background. John was the son of Zebedee and Salome and believed to be younger than his brother James, who also was one of the twelve disciples chosen by Jesus. His mother Salome may have been the sister of Mary, the mother of Jesus (John 19:25). This would have made John a cousin of Jesus and may explain why Jesus, from the cross, chose John to care for his mother rather than Jesus' half brothers. James and John were fishermen like their father and were fishing partners with Peter and Andrew, another pair of brothers, who were also among the twelve disciples of Jesus. Jesus called the brothers, John and James, the Sons of Thunder. They, together with Peter, were close confidants of Jesus and witnessed his transfiguration, where God spoke from a cloud and said, *This is my Son, whom I love. Listen to him!* (Mark 9:7). John felt close to Jesus and referred to himself as the "disciple Jesus loved."

John is believed to have lived longer than any of the other eleven disciples and to have written his manuscripts later than any other writings in the Bible. Bible scholars date his writings around 90 A.D. The Gospels of Matthew, Mark, and Luke are referred to as the Synoptic Gospels because they are literarily similar and may have shared a common source. The Synoptic Gospels tell more of the physical life events and teachings of Jesus. Most scholars date them as written in the 50s or 60s A.D.

John's Gospel has long been thought of as the "Spiritual Gospel." Over 85 percent of the material is unique to John. Since it is thought to have been written many years later, John may have read and had access to the prior Gospels. The accounts of Jesus meeting with Nicodemus and the "Upper Room Discourse" (John 14-17) are important events that were not included in the Synoptic Gospels. Also, John did not include Jesus' genealogy, birth, childhood, temptation, transfiguration, parables, ascension, or even his pronouncement of the Great Commission (to go into all the world and preach the gospel). The only reasonable conclusion is that John was aware of the earlier gospels of Matthew, Mark, and Luke and did not feel the need to repeat the same stories and events.

In the opening paragraph of his gospel, John said about Jesus, *Yet to all that did receive him, to those who believed on his name, he gave the right to become children of God—children not born of natural descent, nor human decision or a husband's will, but born of God* (John 1:12-13). John understood becoming children of God and entering the kingdom of God by being born again by the Spirit. You can trust the teaching in John's gospel about spiritual birth.

John also wrote three letters that are recorded in Scripture. His first letter may have imagined us in his audience. In 1 John 2:12-14, he specifically identified to whom he was writing his letter.

I am writing to you who are God's children
because your sins are forgiven through Jesus.
I am writing to you who are mature in the faith
because you know Christ, who existed from the
beginning.
I am writing to you who are young in the faith
because you have won your battle with the evil
one.
I have written to you who are God's children
because you know the Father.
I have written to you who are mature in the faith
because you know Christ, who existed from the
beginning.
I have written to you who are young in the faith
because you are strong. God's word lives in your
hearts,
and you have won your battle with the evil one.
It is amazing to realize that John is writing
to you personally about being "born again,"
born of God through the Spirit, and becoming
a child of God. John's letter provides a good
depiction of those with spiritual birthdays living
as children of God.

IMAGINING MY AUDIENCE

I would like to imagine that I am writing to the
audience John describes. I'm writing to you who have a
spiritual birthday because your sins have been forgiven on
account of Jesus' name. I'm writing to you, who are young
in the faith, having celebrated few spiritual birthdays,

because God's Word lives in your heart and you have won your battle with the evil one. I'm writing to you, who are mature in the faith, having celebrated many spiritual birthdays, because you know Christ, who existed from the beginning.

I also imagine that there are other readers who do not yet have a spiritual birthday and are not children of God. In John's letter, he points to the differences between those of the world who do not know Christ and those of the kingdom of God. The major difference is: *And this is the testimony: God has given us eternal life, and this life is in his Son. Whoever has the Son has life; whoever does not have the Son of God does not have life* (1 John 5:11-12).

I want to include you who may not yet have a spiritual birthday or who might be unsure if you are spiritually born of God and have eternal life. John made it clear that spiritual birth is not by natural descent. Your parent's faith is not passed on to you as their child. Their dedication or baptism of you as an infant is not your spiritual birth. Baby dedication and infant baptism are expressions of your parent's commendable commitment to God to teach you, with help from the church, about Jesus so you may be born again through the Spirit at a later time.

HOW TO HAVE A SPIRITUAL BIRTH

But you must come to the point where you realize in your mind and heart that your soul is separated from God and that you are spiritually lost. You must recognize God's love and plan for your spiritual birth. It is summarized in John 3:16, *For God so loved the world that he gave his only begotten Son, that whoever believes in him should not perish but have everlasting life.* Jesus came to seek and to save that which was lost. Today, the Holy Spirit is at work seeking and saving the lost. It is important that you respond to the Holy Spirit's calling to change your mind and heart by turning wholeheartedly to God.

Also, repentance plays a critical role in coming to salvation. Repentance may not be a common word in your vocabulary. It is more than feeling bad and then continuing to sin—it is turning away from your sins to follow and honor God with your life. It is changing your mind about Jesus. It is turning from rejection to acceptance—and no past rejection is too big for God's forgiveness. Romans 3:23 tells us that all have sinned and fallen short of God's righteousness. Your repentance must be accompanied by putting your faith in Jesus as your Savior. Saving faith is a spiritual condition of our mind and heart which causes us to trust Jesus alone for eternal life. It must be a personal and sincere faith, and it will result in a continuing spiritual transformation by the Holy Spirit.

Your spiritual birthday is much more amazing and mysterious than your physical birthday. Your physical birth, when you left your mother's womb, changed your external condition. Your spiritual birth, when you place your faith in Christ, changes your internal condition. Once it has happened, you are no longer spiritually lost and separated from God. You are assured that you will see and enter the eternal kingdom of God. You have become a child of God, who is the King of the kingdom. You are baptized in the Holy Spirit, which means at the moment of salvation, the Holy Spirit places you in union with Christ and with other believers in the Body of Christ, the church. The Holy Spirit takes up residence in your life. You are sealed by the Holy Spirit (Ephesians 1:13).

In addition, your name is recorded in Jesus' Book of Life that will be opened in heaven (Revelation 20:12). He is preparing a place there for you for the future, and right now you have thousands of brothers and sisters in Christ here on earth. They will someday be your neighbors in heaven.

The angels in heaven rejoice when you repent and trust in Jesus. As a child of God, you will enjoy the rights and benefits given to all citizens of his kingdom. These are extensive and eternal, and many of them begin on your spiritual birthday. Jesus did not ask the Father to take his disciples out of the world but to protect them from the evil one (John 17:15). Your physical life on earth will continue, and you will have trouble in this world (John 16:33). Your spiritual being, your soul, is safe and securely sealed in Christ by the Holy Spirit (Romans 8:16), which is your advocate to help you and be with you forever. The world cannot accept the Holy Spirit, the Spirit of truth, because it neither sees him nor knows him. But you know him, for he lives with you and will be in you.

SPIRITUAL BIRTH CHECKLIST

If you are still unsure whether you have been born again and have a spiritual birthday, you may use the "R's" checklist.

- You must *reach* the age of accountability when you have knowledge of good and evil.
- You must *realize* that you have a sin nature that separates you from God and that, apart from his help, you are eternally lost.
- You must *recognize* God's plan was to send his Son to die in your place.
- You must *repent* of your sin and turn to God for forgiveness and salvation.
- You must *respond* to God's calling through the Holy Spirit to accept Jesus' sacrificial death and resurrection as payment for your sin.
- You must *receive* him and believe in Jesus to become a child of God. *"Yet to all who did receive him, to those who believed in his name, he gave the right to become children of God"* (John 1:12).
- You may want to confirm your belief and commitment by *reciting* the following prayer.
"Dear Lord Jesus, I know that I am a sinner who needs your salvation, and I ask for your forgiveness. I believe you died for my sins and rose from the dead. I turn from my sins and invite you to come into my life as my Lord and Savior. Please, forgive all my sins, fill me with your Holy Spirit, and begin to lead my life from this day forward. In Jesus' name I pray. Amen."

God does the rest. His Spirit reclaims, redeems, restores, and renews you because of your saving faith in Jesus. Christ's righteousness becomes yours. God promises that you will receive the Holy Spirit at the very moment you give your life to Christ.

It is important to celebrate coming to a saving faith in Christ. Scripture says that the angels of God in heaven rejoice when one person repents (Luke 15:10). If you were genuine in your repentance and faith, God does a miraculous transformation in your spiritual life. You realize that you are born again, and your joy is real. You can rejoice! You have a spiritual birthday to celebrate!

CHAPTER 3

CELEBRATE YOUR SPIRITUAL BIRTHDAY

In the same way, there is joy in the presence of
God's angels whenever one sinner repents.
(Luke 15:10)

Can you imagine not celebrating your physical birthday? Can you imagine not celebrating the most significant day in your life, your spiritual birthday? Can you imagine angels in heaven celebrating your spiritual birthday? Can you imagine every believer in Christ celebrating his or her spiritual birthday every year?

You may not be able to pinpoint the exact date that you responded to God's calling through the Holy Spirit to repentance and receiving Christ. You may, however, be among the many who can recall responding to an invitation by a family member, friend, camp counselor, preacher, or evangelist to pray or make a public confession of your faith. Many born-again believers do not know or recall the exact date that they first believed and professed Christ.

Knowing the date is not as important as knowing that you are born again, From God's perspective, there is a definite point when you trusted in Christ and passed from eternal death into eternal life. A miraculous transformation, empowered by the Holy Spirit, takes place in you as a believer in Christ's redemptive death and resurrection, having "passed from death to life." Christ has recorded it in his Book of Life. From our perspective, a reference point or date for our spiritual birthday is important to commemorate and to celebrate this life-changing event. So "Pick a Date and Celebrate."

PICK A DATE TO CELEBRATE

Picking a date to celebrate your spiritual birthday may reflect an event or time in your life that had a significant role in your spiritual journey to Christ. It may have been a Christian Youth Camp, a visit to a Christian grandparent, or during a crisis in your life. A parent or a believing friend who prayed or helped you cross the line of saving faith may be of help in picking the date. Pick a date to approximate the season or to remember the person who led you to Christ.

You may choose the date of your water baptism as a believer to symbolize your spiritual baptism by the Holy Spirit. It is important to realize that water baptism does not save you. The baptism of the Spirit is necessary for your salvation, and it has nothing to do with water or anything you do or someone else does for you. Baptism by the Spirit is God's gift to you the moment you are born again. Water baptism is an outward physical testimony of an inward spiritual reality that you have personally trusted Christ as your Savior.

The date of your infant baptism should not be chosen as your spiritual birthday. Infant baptism, as practiced by some churches, is a meaningful expression by parents of their desire and commitment to seek God's and the church's help in raising their child. Jesus was dedicated to God by his earthly parents when he was forty days old, as was the Jewish custom. Nowhere in Scripture are infants baptized. An infant or young child under the age of reason cannot make a personal and responsible decision to repent and place their faith in Jesus Christ as their Savior. Jesus taught that little children, who have no knowledge of good or evil, have a special grace and place in heaven. Water baptism of an infant may symbolize membership in a church but not your spiritual birthday.

Confirmation, as practiced by many churches baptizing infants, could be chosen as your spiritual birthday if you personally believed and put your faith in Jesus during this instruction. But many times, the memorization and creeds do not reflect a personal and secure decision of the spiritual mind and heart to trust Jesus as Savior.

REJOICE AND CELEBRATE

You did not get to choose the date of your physical birth, but you can choose the date to celebrate your spiritual birth. Once you do choose the date, celebrate. Do not wait until the next anniversary of your spiritual birthday. Rejoice and celebrate that you now have a spiritual birthday date to celebrate.

So how can you rejoice and celebrate your spiritual birthday to reflect the great sacrifice and commitment Jesus made for your eternal destiny? You can celebrate your second or spiritual birth the same way you celebrate your first or physical birth. You have probably celebrated your physical birth every year since you were physically born. By age two, you were able to recognize that your physical birthday celebration was a special time when you received a lot of birthday gifts and attention from your family and friends. Birthday parties are especially exciting for children. As you attended school and other social activities, you were invited to birthday parties for classmates and friends. Celebrating physical birthdays, both yours and others, became an important part of your childhood memories. Your physical birthday is a time when family and friends come together to celebrate you and your contribution to their lives.

Birthday celebrations are popular in the United States and throughout the entire world. Young and old alike enjoy celebrating their physical birthdays. With a world population of some seven billion people, it is hard to imagine the many ways birthdays are celebrated.

The Bible has little reference to birthday celebrations. Adam lived 930 years but did not have a "birth" day to celebrate. Maybe he celebrated his "created day." Noah celebrated 600 birthdays before the flood. He lived 950 years. Methuselah holds the record for the number of physical birthdays, with 969. His family birthday celebrations must have been very large with so many generations living.

Your spiritual birth is a more important and eternal event in your life than your physical birth. Celebrating your physical birthday will end with your physical death. Celebrating your spiritual birthday will continue for eternity. Only the redeemed, those with a spiritual birthday, will celebrate Jesus in heaven.

How do you celebrate your spiritual birthday? Most occasions have established protocols and traditions on how to celebrate the day. These celebrations may vary by family, nationality, or country. Since the Christian church has not typically celebrated this special day in the life of its members, there are no traditions and few guidelines for celebrating spiritual birthdays.

CELEBRATING MY SPIRITUAL BIRTHDAY

As shared in Chapter 2, my spiritual birthday was November 3, 1960. I had recorded the date in my Bible, but I did not celebrate the annual anniversary as I am proposing now. Not until my fiftieth year in 2010 did I think about celebrating my spiritual birthday. I celebrated the day by taking Martie to lunch at a favorite restaurant and reminiscing about my conversion experience in Sunnyside Baptist church in Los Angeles. I called Warren Smith in California to thank him again for inviting me to his church and to the evangelistic meeting that evening when I made my decision to follow Christ. We have remained friends and in contact over the years since we moved from California. Now I call him every year on my spiritual birthday.

I shared my celebration of fifty years with our pastor, and he announced my milestone to the congregation the following Sunday. Many friends shared congratulatory greetings and shared details of their spiritual birthdays. Most knew "about when" they became believers, but very few knew the actual day. I urged them to "Pick a Date and Celebrate."

I share celebrating my spiritual birthday with my grandchildren. They were interested in hearing my spiritual birthday story and asked questions about the years and events leading to my spiritual birth at age 20. Since I knew that several of the older grandchildren had already accepted Christ as their savior at home or at summer Bible camp, we decided that we should establish an actual or estimated date to celebrate. My oldest daughter had led her children to the Lord at home, and she recorded the actual date. Two grandsons had made their decision to follow Christ at our church Bible camp, so we determined the date of the weeklong camp for those years and picked a day to celebrate.

Since 2011, we have celebrated spiritual birthdays in our family. I found, to my surprise, there are no greeting cards for spiritual birthdays, only cards for physical birthdays with spiritual messages, so I had to improvise and modify cards to reflect a spiritual birthday message. Finding appropriate gifts for a spiritual birthday was not as difficult, as many items with a spiritual message are available. I have given books by Christian authors, Bibles, Christian music, and gift cards. My Christian bookstore has a laser-engraving machine that allowed me to engrave "SPIRITUAL BIRTHDAY" with a person's name and the date on water bottles, key rings, plaques, and wooden boxes. Parents and grandparents remembering and celebrating the spiritual birthdays of their teenage believers may help counter the spiritual falling away that often occurs during these years. Encourage them to celebrate their spiritual birthday with Christian friends and classmates.

ANGELS OF GOD REJOICING IN HEAVEN

Jesus reported in his parable of the lost sheep that when the shepherd returned home, he called together his friends and his neighbors, saying to them, *Rejoice with me, for I have found my sheep that was lost* (Luke 15:6). In the parable of the lost coin, the woman called together her friends and neighbors, saying, *Rejoice with me, for I have found the coin that I had lost* (Luke 15:9). In both parables, Jesus taught that the angels of God in Heaven rejoice and celebrate every sinner that repents. Can you imagine the angels in heaven celebrating your spiritual birthday?

In the parable of the prodigal son, the father closes the story with, *But we had to celebrate and be glad, for this brother of yours was dead and is alive again; he was lost, and is found* (Luke 15:32). Jesus was teaching that it is fitting and important to celebrate and be glad that you are spiritually alive and no longer lost. It is proper for you to celebrate others who were dead and are alive again; they were lost and are found. Call together your friends and neighbors and rejoice together. Celebrating is contagious. Make your spiritual birthday a joyous occasion every year.

PROTOCOL FOR CELEBRATING SPIRITUAL BIRTHDAYS

We have an opportunity to establish the protocol and traditions for celebrating spiritual birthdays. I suggest that you celebrate with prayer, purpose, and passion.

Prayer would be celebrating and thanking your spiritual family in heaven. Thank God, the Father, for your physical creation and for his love in sending his Son to earth so you should "not perish but have eternal life." Thank God, the Son, for suffering, dying, and rising again so that you might be born again and enter the kingdom of God. Thank God, the Holy Spirit, for calling you to salvation through Christ and for living in you. Pray for a filling of the Holy Spirit as you celebrate your spiritual birthday. Pray for and celebrate those who God has used to bring you to faith and those who have helped you grow in your faith. Your prayer may be a private celebration or might be shared with your family and guests at an appropriate time.

The purpose of celebrating your spiritual birthday may seem self-evident but celebrating with purpose will bring greater joy to you and your guests. Let's consider the celebration activities and traditions of other occasions. Physical birthday celebrations, including Jesus' birthday, involve greeting cards, songs, gifts, and cake. These traditions may be adapted or modified to celebrate your second or spiritual birthday. Greeting cards, including e-cards, for birthdays, Christmas, and many and sundry occasions are sent by the millions and can be found in your drugstore, bookstore, or card store. But can you imagine not having one for your spiritual birthday? Hopefully, that will change.

A SPIRITUAL BIRTHDAY SONG

Singing has always been an important way of celebrating together. On your physical birthday, your family and friends have undoubtedly serenaded you with the Happy Birthday song, which is the most recognized song in the English language. Christmas and Easter have many songs, both religious and secular, written to celebrate the occasions. But none of these is as well-known as the Happy Birthday song:

> *Happy Birthday to you, Happy Birthday to you,*
> *Happy Birthday dear (your name), Happy Birthday to you.*

Year after year, this simple song has been your physical birthday celebration song. In 1893, Patty Hill, a kindergarten principal, together with her sister Mildred, a pianist and composer, wrote new lyrics to the melody of *"Good Morning to All"* for their kindergarten students. Those kindergarteners taught others the simple song that is sung for you each year. The lyrics have been translated into more than 18 languages. Several countries have added traditional sayings immediately after *Happy Birthday* is sung.

The word "happy" is not used often in Scripture, while "joy" and "rejoice" are used hundreds of times. Angel announced Jesus birthday to shepherds saying; *Do not be afraid. I bring you good news of great joy that will be for all the people. Today in the town of David a Savior has been born to you;*

he is Christ, the Lord (Luke 2:10-11). Jesus said, *I have told you this so that my joy may be in you, and that your joy may be complete* (John 15:11).

"Have a joyous birthday" may be a preferred greeting for a spiritual birthday. Your celebration song could simply modify the lyrics to:

"Joyous *Birthday to you, Joyous Birthday to you, Joyous Birthday dear (your name)., Joyous Birthday to you."*

My suggestion for a more appropriate spiritual birthday song is a modification of the chorus of the old hymn written by Philip Doddridge in 1755, *"O Happy Day":*

Joyous Day, Joyous Day, When Jesus washed your sins away!
He's in your heart to live and stay, and we rejoice with you today.
Joyous Day, Joyous Day, It's (your name)'s spiritual birthday!

It does reflect the reason for your spiritual birthday and for the celebration.

SPIRITUAL BIRTHDAY CELEBRATION TRADITIONS

Your physical birthday celebrations are usually centered on you, with gifts showered on you by others. Jesus' physical birthday is celebrated by the giving and receiving of gifts by your family and friends. The origin of giving gifts at Christmas is unclear, like its date. Christians interpret the tradition to represent the three Magi giving gifts of frankincense, gold, and myrrh to the baby Jesus.

Your spiritual birthday celebration is an opportunity to focus on others and on Jesus. You may want to give or channel gifts to a favorite ministry or charity. You may want to send greetings or a note of appreciation to those who have impacted your spiritual life. You may decide to have a party or celebration with others with special physical or spiritual needs. Jesus said, *I tell you the truth, whatever you did for one of the least of these brothers and of mine, you did for me* (Matthew 25:11). Celebrating with your friends and with other friends of Jesus may make your spiritual birthday party more joyful for you now and may result in others rejoicing in eternity.

Another tradition at physical birthday celebrations is a cake with candles.

The exact origin and significance of traditions related to cake and candles at birthday celebrations are unknowns and vary from country to country.

You may want to consider candles for their significance in Scripture. Jesus said,

> *Neither do people light a lamp and put under a bowl. Instead they put it on its stand, and it gives light to everyone in the house. In the same way, let your light shine before men, that they may see your deeds and praise your Father in heaven.* **(Matthew 5:15-16)**

The lighting of the candles and cutting of the cake may provide a good time to let your light shine. Your spiritual birthday differs from your physical birthday in ways that you may wish to celebrate. Although you were present at your physical birth, you don't remember the experience—but you remember and can share your spiritual birthday story with your guests.

Physical births are all very similar, but each spiritual birth has a unique story as to God's calling. It is important to know your own spiritual birthday story well enough to retell it. The primary value of knowing and telling the story of your spiritual birth is for your own appreciation of the depth of God's love for us. You can share about God's grace in your life before, during, and after your spiritual birthday. Since your spiritual life is an unfinished story, you can share your spiritual growth and assurances of God's leading in your life. Too often in testimonies, we talk about ourselves and how we found God rather than how God found us. Use your spiritual birthday to share your story in a natural and winsome way, giving God the praise.

CELEBRATE YOUR SPIRITUAL BIRTHDAY WITH PASSION

Celebrate your spiritual birthday with passion. Emotion is a very basic element of celebrations. Your spiritual birthday should bring strong emotions of joy and hope for your future. You were spiritually dead and now you are alive. You have eternal life in heaven and have avoided spiritual death. Your old life has passed away and all things are new. You are a child of God. You are not celebrating a new year; you are celebrating a new life in Christ.

We can get very passionate about celebrating a football team's victory or a rock star's concert. Many occasions that we celebrate with passion are soon over and forgotten. Consider the very first spiritual birthday celebration on Pentecost Sunday when thousands of Jews, devout men from every nation under heaven living in Jerusalem, heard the rushing wind of the Holy Spirit and came together to hear Peter proclaim the good news that God had made Jesus both Lord and Savior. About 3000 responded to the invitation to repent and be baptized in the name of Jesus Christ and were born again. Three thousand souls experienced their spiritual birth that day. They were from every known region and spoke many different languages yet began to celebrate together with passion.

These born-again believers were no longer strangers but brothers and sisters in Christ, and they began to celebrate together. This was not cake and candles, but all the believers were together and had everything in common.

> *They devoted themselves to the apostles' teaching and to fellowship, to breaking of bread and to prayer. Everyone was filled with awe at the many wonders and signs performed by the apostles. They broke bread in their homes and ate together with glad and sincere hearts, praising God and enjoying the favor of all the people. And the Lord added to their number daily those who were being saved.* (Acts 2:42-47)

It sounds to me like they were celebrating spiritual birthdays—their own, and the many additional people who were being added to the church family each day!

Celebrating your spiritual birthday with passion can be very contagious. Others will want to join with you in celebrating and rejoicing. A large celebration is always attractive to both young and old. Be a contagious celebrating Christian enjoying and sharing your spiritual birthday.

CELEBRATE WITH YOUR CHURCH FAMILY

You cannot expect your modern-day church to celebrate exactly like the early church in Jerusalem, but their spirit of unity, fellowship, outreach, and prayer can certainly be celebrated in your church. Your church needs to be a place where you fellowship and celebrate each other. The fellowship among born-again believers celebrating together is contagious to members and non-members of the church. The world does not view the Christian church as people celebrating each other as brothers and sisters in Christ. You and other members celebrating God and each other will be attractive to visitors and seekers. You have so much to celebrate because of your spiritual birthday. Rejoice and celebrate with your fellow believers on earth. You will be preparing for celebrating together forever with Jesus in heaven.

How you celebrate your spiritual birthday is limited only by your imagination and resources. You are celebrating being the child of an unlimited God, eternal life with God rather than eternal death separated from God. Celebrate the indwelling of the Holy Spirit in you now and forever. Rejoice and celebrate the most miraculous and incomprehensible gift of God's grace to you. Celebrate your spiritual birthday with prayer, purpose, and passion.

CHAPTER 4

CELEBRATE
YOUR SPIRITUAL JOURNEY

"For I know the plans I have for you," says the Lord.
"They are plans for good and not for disaster,
to give you a future and a hope."
(Jeremiah 29:11)

Can you imagine not celebrating major events or accomplishments on your life's journey? Can you remember as a child celebrating your physical growth and abilities in sports, music, or games? Celebrating is a big part of your journey on earth. Graduations, weddings, promotions, reunions, and retirement are major celebrations and milestones on your physical journey. Unlike other journeys, reaching your physical journey's destination is not an anticipated big celebration. Solomon, who had great wisdom and wealth, celebrated many physical successes and pleasures but concluded that all were meaningless and that death was mankind's destination. His final words were, *Now all has been heard: here is the conclusion of the matter: Fear God and keep his commandments, for this is the whole duty of man* (Ecclesiastes 12:13).

The spiritual journey of mankind is recorded and revealed in Scripture. The Bible describes mankind's journey from the beginning in the Garden of Eden to the end in "a new heaven and new earth" when Jesus returns for his bride, the church. It breaks mankind's spiritual journey into three periods; before Christ, Christ's life on earth, and after Christ. The Old Testament books were preparing God's people for the coming of a Messiah or Savior. The four Gospels record Jesus's life, death, and resurrection to provide for mankind's salvation. The balance of the New Testament records the workings of the Holy Spirit and the early church to spread the good news to the entire world. Mankind's spiritual journey continues through the works of the church and the Holy Spirit until Christ returns.

CELEBRATE YOUR NEW LIFE

Can you imagine your spiritual journey having three similar periods? Before Christ, separated from God and seeking a Savior; your spiritual birthday, when you received and believed in Christ as your Savior; and now new life with the Holy Spirit guiding you. You can look forward to celebrating your spiritual journey and destination forever.

The first thing to celebrate is that, spiritually, you belong to Christ and have become a new person. The old life is gone; a new life has begun. A good way to celebrate this new life is through believer's baptism by immersion, which is a physical representation of your new spiritual beginning. It symbolizes your old self being buried with

Christ and rising with him to become a new creature. It is a celebration that you may share with your family, your friends, and your church. It is a proclamation of your saving faith in God. It is also a physical representation of your spiritual baptism by the Holy Spirit. If your church does not baptize adults by immersion, find a pastor who will baptize you. You may be baptized in a swimming pool, lake, river, or even a horse tank.

SPIRITUAL INFANTS

God does not abandon you after your spiritual birth. You are his child, and He gives you his Spirit to live within you to care for you. Much like a mother is there for her infant child, the Spirit is there to care for each infant child of God. Depending upon your knowledge of Jesus and the Bible before your spiritual birth, your spiritual growth can be rapid or slow.

Most new spiritual infants crave spiritual milk to satisfy their desire to know more about Jesus and their new life. Your church or a mature Christian mentor can provide this spiritual milk. If you do not attend church, it is important to find a good Bible-believing church that has programs and materials for teaching and growing new believers in their faith walk. Many new born-again believers are not fed and taught the basic truths of Scripture and, therefore, do not grow in their spiritual journey with Christ.

SPIRITUAL GROWTH

As on your physical journey, these early months and years lay the spiritual foundation needed to build future spiritual growth. You must also pursue your spiritual growth with prayer, purpose, and passion. You need to learn the elementary truths of God's Word and teachings about righteousness. By daily prayer, studying the Bible, seeking instruction, and applying spiritual truth, you will experience and celebrate spiritual growth. Attend your church regularly to worship God and learn how to draw closer to him. Join a Bible study or small community group of believers to share your growth. Each Sunday can be a celebration of God and your spiritual formation. Scripture promises that the Spirit of God will give you the ability to understand the things of God. Pray that the Holy Spirit will reveal God's teachings and wisdom to you. Your spiritual mind and heart must learn to love God. His teachings will benefit you on both your spiritual and physical journeys.

SPIRITUAL GIFTS

God wants you to become a contributing citizen of his kingdom on earth; therefore, the Holy Spirit will give you spiritual gifts to benefit the body of Christ. Gifts of the Spirit are described in the following chapters: Romans 12, 1 Corinthians 12, and Ephesians 5. They include discernment, exhortation, evangelism, faith, giving, guidance, help/serving, knowledge, leadership, mercy, teaching/preaching, and wisdom. Spiritual gifts are given to the church through its members as needed. Your church should help you discover and develop your spiritual gift or gifts. Your church may use a spiritual gifts questionnaire or test to help determine your gifts. If they do not, there are spiritual gifts surveys online. The goal is not simply discovering your spiritual gifts but knowing how to best serve God within the church body.

SPIRITUAL WORKS

Celebrate your spiritual gifts by serving in ministries that need your gifts. Jesus commissioned his disciples to witness to and care for his people. As a born-again believer, you are called to do God's work on earth. However, works do not save you; Jesus does. Spiritual works will result from your saving faith and changed heart.

Jesus said that whatever good works we have done to others, we have done for him. In his letter to the early church, James, the brother of Jesus, wrote,

> *In the same way, faith by itself, if it is not accompanied by action, is dead. But, someone will say, "You have faith, I have deeds." Show me your faith without deeds, and I will show you my faith by what I do* (James 2:17-18).

I have always liked James' wisdom and practical instruction for our spiritual works and journey.

SPIRITUAL INVESTING

Your spiritual gifts and works will allow you to make spiritual investments. Jesus, in his parable of the talents, indicated that he expects a return on his investment in us. If we bury our talents rather than investing them for his kingdom's gain, we will not hear: *Well done, good and faithful servant! You have been faithful over a few things; I will put you in charge of many things. Come and share your master's happiness* (Matthew 25:22). In his Sermon on the Mount, Jesus preached,

> *Do not store up for yourselves treasures on earth, where moth and rust destroy, and where thieves break in and steal. But store up for yourselves treasures in heaven, where moth and rust do not destroy, and thieves do not break in and steal. For where your treasure is, there your heart will be also.* **(Matthew 6:19-21)**

Your spiritual investments will return eternal benefits for you.

You will not have to wait until heaven to experience the benefits of your spiritual works and investments. Just as you receive and celebrate the fruits of your physical labor, you will receive fruits of the Spirit for your spiritual labor. The fruit of the Spirit is more desirable than money, cars, homes, and other physical possessions. Paul explained in his letter to the Galatians, *But the fruit of the Spirit is love, joy, peace, patience, kindness, goodness, faithfulness, gentleness, and self- control. Against such things there is no law* **(Galatians 5:22-26)**.

SPIRITUAL WARFARE

Paul also describes the spiritual warfare you will experience on your journey in his letter to the Ephesians:

> *Finally, be strong in the Lord and in the strength of his might. Put on the whole armor of God, that you may be able to stand against the schemes of the devil. For we do*

not wrestle against flesh and blood, but against the rulers, against the authorities, against the cosmic powers over this present darkness, against the spiritual forces of evil in the heavenly places. Therefore take up the whole armor of God, that you may be able to withstand in the evil day, and having done all, to stand firm. Stand therefore, having fastened on the belt of truth, and having put on the breastplate of righteousness, and as shoes for your feet, having put on the readiness given by the gospel of peace. In all circumstances, take up the shield of faith, with which you can extinguish all the flaming darts of the evil one. Take the helmet of salvation, and the sword of the Spirit, which is the word of God. Praying at all times in the Spirit, with all prayer and supplication **(Ephesians 6:10-18).**

You must be ready for spiritual warfare on your spiritual journey. Remember that you war not against flesh and blood but the spiritual forces of evil. In these evil days we live in, sometimes we think the enemy is our neighbor rather than Satan and his evil schemes. Jesus won the war for us on the cross, but Satan has not fully surrendered. God has provided you a set of armor so you can stand firm against the attacks of evil and do battle with the sword of the Spirit to win souls. The truth, the righteousness, and the gospel of Jesus provide you protection against the rulers, authorities, and powers of this dark world. When the attacks of Satan come, you must rely on your saving faith and salvation in Christ to ward off the flaming arrows and take up the Word of God as your weapon. Put on the whole armor of God and stand firm in your faith in him during your spiritual warfare against the evil one.

We really do not know God's plans for our physical journey or our spiritual journey. You will plan physical journeys to various physical destinations during your life on earth. You may be old enough to remember planning automobile journeys on paper roadmaps and comparing routes to your destination. Now most automobile journeys are planned using GPS technology on a smartphone or built-in navigation equipment. The Global Positioning System was developed in the 1980s utilizing satellites circling the globe. GPS devices can pinpoint your physical location, determine possible routes for your journey, and track where you are geographically as you travel to your destination. When you deviate from your planned route, it will inform you and recalculate new directions to put you back on your planned journey.

YOUR SPIRITUAL JOURNEY GPS

Your GPS on your spiritual journey is God's Positioning Spirit. Long before satellite technology, God placed a GPS in each new believer in Jesus on his or her spiritual birthday. Jesus, who is your first advocate, sent a second advocate, the Holy Spirit, after his ascension to heaven. You will encounter many rough spots, potholes, and detours on your spiritual journey in this world. You can rely on the power and protection of the Spirit to guide and carry you through to your destination.

In addition to God's Positioning Spirit, God provides a detailed travel guide for your spiritual journey on earth, known as the Bible. The Bible begins with laws and commandments to guide you on your journey. It includes actual stories of many of his chosen people's journeys. The Old Testament stories and journeys led to the coming of Jesus and his physical journey on earth.

JESUS' PRAYER, PURPOSE, AND PASSION

Jesus came to fulfill the law and to open wide the way to eternal life through his death and resurrection. In his human life on earth, Jesus received power through the Spirit to carry out the will of the Father. The Holy Spirit descended on Jesus at his baptism by John the Baptist. Throughout his journey on earth, he ministered in the power of the Spirit. Jesus demonstrated prayer, purpose, and passion in his mission and ministry to seek and to save what was lost. Jesus prayed often during his journey on earth, but few of his prayers were written down. His recorded prayers were spoken with purpose and passion. Hebrews 5:7 records, *During the days of Jesus' life on earth, he offered up prayers and petitions with fervent cries and tears to the one who could save him from death, and he was heard because of his reverent submission.*

Jesus pursued his purpose on earth with prayer and passion. He prayed for God's will to be done on earth as it is in heaven. He knew his purpose was to seek and to save the lost and to serve God, which he did with passion and love for the lost. Jesus had passion, with prayer and purpose. His love for the people was demonstrated in his prayers, preaching and healing their every disease and sickness. His ultimate passion was taking our sins upon himself and dying on the cross. His great love and purpose was to give us eternal life. Jesus' journey on earth is a major section of God's travel guide for your spiritual journey. Four books of the Bible by four writers emphasize his important role in providing the way for you to reach the kingdom of heaven. His prayer, purpose, and passion were for you to be there with him.

The balance of the guide (the New Testament) explains God's new covenant and direction for your spiritual journey, with stories about the acts of the apostles and the early church. It includes letters to the early churches giving encouragement and teachings to help them on their spiritual journeys. The spiritual advice and wisdom in this section of the guide can be very helpful to you on your journey. Your spiritual journey in this world is very short compared to your eternal journey with Christ. Celebrate your spiritual journey with prayer, purpose, and passion as you travel to your destination and your Big Celebration.

CHAPTER 5

SHARING YOUR SPIRITUAL BIRTHDAY STORY

Always be prepared to give an answer to everyone who
asks you to give the reason for the hope that you have.
1 Peter 3:15

Can you imagine discovering the cure for a fatal disease but not sharing it with those inflicted by it? Sin is a fatal disease. You were exposed to sin and contracted the contagious disease. Without a cure, you were facing eternal death. Fortunately, through the work of the Great Physician, Jesus, you were able to find the cure. Jesus took your sin upon himself and suffered and died in your place so that you could live and have eternal life. The good news is that the cure is also contagious, and you must share the cure with others who have the disease. Having a spiritual birthday for a non-believer is a life-or-death matter. Without saving faith in Jesus, people face eternal death.

Jesus was planning your spiritual birthday when he went to the cross. It was a life-or-death decision, and he chose death to give you eternal life. Christ died for our sins in accordance with the Scriptures. *For God so loved the world, that he gave his only Son that whosoever believes in him shall not perish but have eternal life.* This is the good news story for all mankind. You must see lost people like Jesus did, with love and compassion. You must share his teaching that "You must be born again," It is important that they know they must be born of the Spirit.

THE GREAT COMMISSION

Jesus, after his resurrection, commissioned his disciples saying:

> *All authority in heaven and on earth has been given to me. Therefore, go and make disciples of all nations, baptizing them in the name of the Father, and of the Son and of the Holy Spirit, and teach them to obey everything I commanded you. And surely I am with you always, to the very end of the age.* **(Matthew 28:16-20)**

Luke records in Acts 1:8 how Jesus, just moments before his ascension into heaven, explains his "being with us always," saying: *But you will receive power when the Holy Spirit comes on you, and you will be my witnesses in Jerusalem, and in all Judea and Samaria, and to the ends of the earth.*

Jesus continues to have all authority in heaven and on earth. He commands us to go and make disciples of all nations. His promise of power through the Holy Spirit continues for us today and until the end of the age. The world has changed in the two thousand years since Jesus ascended, but the Great Commission and the power of the Holy Spirit have not changed. The Jerusalem, Judea, Samaria, and world that Jesus and the disciples knew have changed over the centuries.

Billions have believed in the name of Jesus and have entered the kingdom of heaven. But as Jesus explained:

> *Enter through the narrow gate. For wide is the gate and broad is the road that leads to destruction and many enter through it. But small is the gate and narrow the road that leads to life, and only a few find it.* (Matthew 7:13-14)

This prediction should not discourage you from sharing your spiritual birthday story but encourage you to share the good news of how Jesus provided the narrow way for you. Peter wrote concerning Jesus' second coming:

> *But do not overlook this one fact, that with the Lord one day is as a thousand years, and a thousand years as one day. The Lord is not slow to fulfill his promise as some count slowness, but is patient toward you, not wishing that any should perish, but that all should reach repentance.* (2 Peter 3:9)

SENT OUT BY JESUS

We need to recognize the urgency of being Jesus' witnesses to this dying world. He prayed, *They are not of the world, even as I am not of it. Sanctify them by the truth; your word is truth. As you sent them into the world, I send them into the world* (John 17:16-18).

His prayer was not that the Father take us out of the world, but that the Father would protect us from the evil one. He is sending you into the world to testify that God sent Jesus to seek and save that which was lost. Jesus promised to send the Holy Spirit to be our advocate, and he gave his peace to us so we would not be troubled or afraid. It is important, when sharing your spiritual birthday story, to remember the Holy Spirit is in charge, and he will help you find the right words. The real work belongs to God's Spirit, who convicts the world of the need for a savior, changes people's hearts, and transforms people.

Your part is to share the good news about Jesus. Sharing your spiritual birthday story can be a very natural and exciting experience when you realize the result will cause both you and the angels in heaven to rejoice and celebrate. Spiritual birth is really an eternal life or eternal death matter. Understanding the eternal consequences of not having saving faith in Jesus and experiencing God's amazing grace should be incentives to share your spiritual birthday story with all your family and friends. Share your spiritual birthday story with prayer, purpose, and passion.

SHARING WITH PRAYER

Prayer is the unseen cornerstone of sharing your spiritual birthday story. You unleash the power of the Holy Spirit when you pray for lost people. The Spirit will hear and answer your prayers asking for a spiritual birthday for another person. Pray for yourself and for others to help you share the importance of a spiritual birthday. There are many ways to pray for people who are spiritually lost. Pray for individuals you know by name as you are reminded of them. Pray for them when you see them, when you drive past their home, or as you have contact through social media. Praying for an unbeliever when they are ill, under stress or sorrow, and seeking your counsel can be an effective way to initiate a spiritual relationship or discussion.

Praying with them and seeking God's blessing and guidance for them will open future opportunities to share the gospel with them. Continue to pray for their needs and follow up to show your concern. Pray that God will not only meet their needs but that the Holy Spirit will convict them of sin and their need for God's grace. Pray with passion for their spiritual birth. Your love and concern for their physical and spiritual well-being may require a long season of prayer to see a spiritual birthday.

SHARING WITH PURPOSE

Your purpose is to be Jesus' witness and share the good news. It is the Holy Spirit who brings conviction and the spiritual birth of his children.

The purpose of sharing your spiritual birthday story is to bring someone to a saving faith in Jesus. You must plan your story to reach people where they are in their physical and spiritual journeys. You often do not know the spiritual condition of the person's heart. This is why it is important to pray for and to prepare children during their young and innocent years so that when they reach the age of reason and accountability, they are prepared to make a decision to follow Christ. After their years of innocence, they may be influenced by the world's culture and education system. For a teenager, hearing and observing your spiritual story can be very helpful in bring direction into their physical, moral, and spiritual lives. They may have heard the good news of Jesus, but now they must trust in him, thus turning it into their spiritual birthday story. Planting seeds for spiritual birth early in this season of life will usually result in a bountiful harvest.

The Apostle Paul explained to the Corinthians, *I planted the seed, Apollos watered it, but God has been making it grow. So neither the one who plants nor the one waters anything, but only God, who makes things grow* (1 Corinthians 3:6-7). You may prepare the soil and plant the seed, or you may water what another has planted. But remember that only God, through the Holy Spirit, gives spiritual birth.

SHARING OTHERS' SPIRITUAL BIRTHDAY STORIES

Your spiritual birthday story most likely includes other believers' stories that prepared the soil, planted, and watered the seed that the Holy Spirit used in giving you spiritual birth. I can trace my story back to a spiritual birthday story in 1946 that influenced my spiritual birth years later. My future brother-in-law, Orland, was a young sailor serving in the navy stationed in Memphis, Tennessee. His chief petty officer shared his spiritual birthday story and invited him to attend an old-fashioned revival meeting in the city auditorium featuring the Reverend Charles E. Fuller, a well-known radio preacher.

At the end of the evening, when an invitation was given to repent and believe in Jesus Christ as their Lord and Savior, the young sailor raised his hand and Fuller called him forward to speak with a counselor. He was born again unto eternal life. The date of his spiritual birthday was October 9, 1946.

A few months later, in April 1947, he was home on leave and shared his spiritual birthday experience with his family, including four younger sisters. One sister, Martie, my future wife, listened with much interest to her brother's story. All the children had learned much about the good news story from their born-again mother, but ten-year-old Martie had not made a personal decision to follow Christ. Her brother shared more about spiritual birth and, with tears flowing, she decided to repent and ask Jesus to enter her life as Savior. She did not record her spiritual birth, and years later was unable to remember the date. Since it was near her brother's birthday, she picked April 16, 1947 to celebrate her spiritual birthday.

My spiritual birthday story was greatly influenced by my wife's spiritual birthday story. Many years later, she went down the aisle to reconfirm her faith and rededicate her life to Christ. I followed her down the aisle to put my faith in Jesus and receive him as my personal Savior and Lord.

SHARING WITH PASSION

Sharing your spiritual birthday story must be done with passion. Your passion to share the good news of Jesus is essential to achieving your purpose to lead others into the kingdom of heaven. When you realize that a person's eternal destination may depend on you sharing the truth you received through God's grace, you should be moved to action. Sharing your heart's deep love and passion for Jesus with people who are spiritually disconnected should come naturally.

We tend to share what we are passionate about. It may be a sports team, a performer, a band, a new child, a hobby, and the list goes on. As born-again believers, we have a responsibility to steward our passion for Jesus and keep our hearts burning hot and our lives engaged in reaching out to the lost. Effective outreach is not a system, a program, or a specific presentation. It starts with your love for God and for others. People need to hear about God's love and grace, but they also need to see it in you. As his witness and ambassador on earth, you are to reflect his love, his grace, and his passion for mankind wherever, whenever, however, and to whomever the Spirit leads. How you live and celebrate your spiritual life must reflect the presence and power of the Spirit living within you. People will see in you a joy and a passion for life that they are seeking.

GOD IN YOUR STORY

You must be prepared to share your faith and the story of how God is working in your life. Spiritual conversations do not have to be forced or uncomfortable. They can be a natural part of your daily life. God wants your faith to overflow into your interactions and conversations with people. If your faith is real, people will recognize your passion and be drawn to it. Be ready to share your testimony of God's working in your life. Talk about your spiritual birthday and how it changed your life. Have a short version that you can expand as appropriate. Make God's presence and power central to your story.

Try to relate your testimony to your listener's areas of interest, questions, or needs. If you have been in a similar situation, your experience and God's answer may be timely. Encourage questions and responses to your story. Ask questions so you may respond to their feelings and concerns. Be sensitive to their readiness and desire to hear and respond to the gospel message of Jesus. Be prepared to share this life-changing message of salvation in a clear and compelling way. The key is to have the gospel deep in your heart so you are ready to express it in ways that will connect naturally with the one you are sharing it with. There is only one gospel but many ways to express it.

Hearing other Christians share their spiritual birthday stories is always inspiring and encouraging. Many organized churches have abandoned testimony services where members share their spiritual birthday stories and other workings of the Spirit in their lives. Every born-again Christian has a spiritual birthday story, and everyone is different. Every story reinforces the power of the gospel through the Holy Spirit to change lives. Stories shared help listeners imagine and understand the many ways the Spirit works in an individual with different backgrounds and questions.

MARK'S SPIRITUAL BIRTHDAY STORY

Telling other Christians' spiritual birthday stories, especially when you were part of the story, can often be helpful to demonstrate that each spiritual birth is unique.

Your knowledge of your family members' stories can help bridge generational and cultural differences. My nephew Mark, son of Orland, has a unique spiritual birthday story that might resonate with many young people.

His Christian parents loved the Lord and served their local church faithfully. They taught their four children Bible stories, Scripture verses, and how to pray. They took them to Sunday school and church services every Sunday. As a child, Mark loved Jesus and enjoyed being with his family and friends at church. In high school, though, he began to drift away from God and the church.

After high school, while working in a local music store, a friend asked, "So, Mark, are you a Christian?"

Mark answered, "Sure, Terry, I'm a Christian. Why do you ask?"

Terry challenged Mark, saying, "How can you call yourself a Christian and yet do so many things that Christians don't do?"

Mark wasn't sure what to say, but finally responded, "Well, I guess I'm just a *cool* Christian."

"Oh, really?" Terry quickly countered. "Don't you know there's a term for cool Christians?" Without hesitating, Terry answered his own question. *"Hypocrites!"*

This made Mark angry, but later he realized his friend was right. This encounter, combined with sobering conversations with his father, the prayers of his grandmother and other family members, the godly examples of Christian friends who were part of a weekly Bible study, an evangelistic message Mark listened to on a cassette tape, and a variety of other influences finally got through to him. While driving alone on a rural highway, he repented and asked God to forgive him and to take control of his life. He committed to following Christ from that evening on November 8, 1976 all the way into eternity. He came alive spiritually and soon found himself following new marching orders from God as he pursued a college education and later a seminary degree, all of which led him to full-time service for Jesus.

Mark Mittelberg has shared his spiritual birthday story with thousands of people over the years through speaking, books, and one-on-one conversations. You may have heard him speak or have read his books, including the bestselling book and training course, *Becoming a Contagious Christian*. Some of his published materials are listed in the Resources section of this book.

LEE'S SPIRITUAL BIRTHDAY STORY

Immediately after finishing seminary, Mark joined the staff of a large church in the Chicago area as their director of evangelism. On his very first day there, Mark was introduced to Lee, who had also joined the church staff that day, assigned to lead in an administrative role and help Mark in the area of evangelism. Since Mark and Lee would be working together, they spent some time getting acquainted. Lee shared that he had come to Christ on November 8, 1981. Mark responded that he had come to Christ in November as well but could not recall the exact date—but he knew he had it recorded in his Bible. Mark went to get his Bible only to find, to his amazement,

82 | YOUR SPIRITUAL BIRTHDAY

that they shared spiritual birthdays—November 8, exactly five years apart!

Already brothers in Christ, they became best friends and partners in ministry, and they have now celebrated their spiritual birthdays together for more than thirty years.

Lee's spiritual birthday story was much different from Mark's. Lee had a journalism degree from the University of Missouri and a legal studies degree from Yale Law School. He had been an award-winning legal editor for the Chicago Tribune. Lee's spiritual birthday story began when his wife, Leslie, came home one day and shared her brand-new spiritual birth story. Her neighbor had previously shared her spiritual birthday story and invited Leslie to go to church with her (ironically, to the church where Mark and Lee met years later as new staff members).

When Leslie told Lee she had received Christ, his response was anger and hostility. He had some knowledge of the Bible from his upbringing but now considered himself an atheist. He believed God was a product of mythology or wishful thinking. More than that, Lee had little interest in being married to a Christian, and their love story—which had begun in high school—was in real jeopardy. But over time, Lee noted a subtle but significant shift in Leslie's attitude as a Christian. Lee decided to investigate the claims of Christianity in order to get the facts on what he considered false beliefs and teachings. For nearly two years, he applied his legal training and experience as a seasoned journalist to prove his case. He investigated and weighed the evidence from experts in the fields of history, science, and theology, all in the effort to scrutinize and, he hoped, undermine the credibility of Christianity.

To make a long story short, Lee accumulated evidence that pointed so powerfully toward the truth of Christianity that on November 8, 1981, he finally acknowledged that Jesus was the Son of God who was crucified for our sins and rose from the dead to provide us with eternal life. He received God's gift of salvation by putting his faith in Jesus as his Forgiver and Leader. Lee became a born again Christian.

Later, Lee Strobel wrote a book about his extended spiritual birthday story, titled *The Case for Christ*. It became a *New York Times* bestseller, with nearly five million copies sold. More recently, a full-length movie with the same title was made, portraying those two years of his spiritual birthday story and its impact on his relationship with Leslie. You may have seen the movie or read one of Lee's books. They are also listed in the Resources section.

INCLUDE THE GOSPEL MESSAGE

You may not become a full-time speaker and writer like Mark or Lee, or have a movie made of your spiritual birthday story. However, you can tell your story to others like Orland's navy friend and Leslie's neighborhood friend did, leading to life-changing spiritual birthdays for them and perhaps others. We all can share our story and the good news of Jesus with friends, family, coworkers, or classmates. To do so effectively, though, you must be prepared to share not only your spiritual birthday story but also the gospel message. You may be familiar with a specific gospel presentation using Scriptures or other tools. You may want to study and understand several approaches that you can adapt to your particular situation. The Roman Road is a step-by-step look at key verses in the book of Romans that present the truths of the faith. You just need a Bible or Bible app on your phone that is marked with the verses and sequence (a simple version includes these three verses: Romans 3:23, 6:23, and 10:13).

Another presentation called the Bridge to Life involves drawing a simple sketch of a stick person and God separated by a wide ravine titled sin and death. The only way to get over the ravine to God's side is by way of the cross, which forms a bridge with the vertical line through the words sin and death and the horizontal line bridging the gap between the unbeliever and God. Small tracts are also available that present the gospel with Scripture and drawings that allow you to easily share the plan of salvation.

If you are unsure of a person's spiritual condition, you can ask them, "When is your spiritual birthday?" If they do not understand the term, you have an opportunity to share the need for a second birth. Remember Nicodemus, who was a very religious person, but did not understand how he could be born again. If they understand the term but are not sure if they have a spiritual birthday, you can explain that knowing Jesus personally is the only way to be sure of spiritual birth. If they know that have a spiritual birthday but do not know the date, help them pick a date and celebrate.

Sharing a gospel presentation can become an adventure. In addition to your prayer, purpose, and passion, use your imagination. Every person is unique, so your sharing must be flexible and creative. Each spiritual birth is different and requires your Spirit-anointed ingenuity.

Adapt your presentation to the person's temperament, background, interests, and responses. Imagine you are a fisher of men and what fishing techniques, equipment, lures, and time it will take to land this man. Imagine you are a football coach and which offensive plays you will call against his defense. Imagine you are a salesperson and how you will close the sale against your competition, knowing you have exactly what your client needs.

BE PERSISTENT BUT PATIENT

You may imagine quick success, but the growing season may be much longer than imagined. Keep planting seeds and watering the soil. Keep casting your line or net and trying new lures. Keep calling new plays and making a few yards. Keep in contact and try new sales techniques on your client. God is responsible through the Spirit for the results. The harvest, the catch, the touchdown, or sale is the Lord's. You may not know the final results this side of heaven.

Sharing the gospel is much more than planting a garden, a fishing trip, a football game, or another sale. Imagine it as fighting a war. You are actually engaged in spiritual warfare for the souls of men and women. The stakes are high and the battle is intense. Jesus provides the way for victory, but the battle continues. If you have a spiritual birthday, you have won your battle over spiritual death through Jesus' death and resurrection. You are taking the offense in the battle for the person's eternal soul. If Christians do not take a stand against Satan, many souls will be lost to eternal separation from God. The church of born-again believers is God's army against the forces of evil. You must stay alert and always keep praying in the Spirit. Jesus has sent us into the world to do battle for souls. He sent the Holy Spirit to lead and protect us in the battle.

Remember your own spiritual birthday. Your life was changed, and you have the hope of eternal life with Jesus. Your experience should motivate your desire for everyone to have a spiritual birthday like yours. You will be able to celebrate together forever.

SHARING MY SPIRITUAL BIRTHDAY STORY

Before Christ:

Born Again:

After Decision:

CHAPTER 6

THE CHURCH'S ROLE

"He who has an ear, let him hear
what the Spirit says to the churches."
(Revelation 2: 7, 11, 17 & 20; 3: 6, 13 & 22)

The English word "church" has several meanings or images. Do you imagine a physical building with a steeple that you often see as you travel? Or do you imagine an hour-long service that you attend on Sunday mornings? You may imagine a specific congregation of a specific denomination at a specific location, which you consider your church.

The Greek word, *ekklesia*, meaning "called out" has been translated as "church" in English Bibles. The church is the called-out community of God's redeemed people who have truly trusted Christ alone for their salvation. It is created by the Holy Spirit to exalt Jesus Christ as Lord of all. The bond between its members is their common spiritual birth as children of God.

There is ultimately only one church, the global community of believers on earth plus those already in glory. Theologians distinguish between the "visible church" (the church as Christians on earth see it) and the "invisible church" (the church as God in heaven sees it). This distinction emphasizes that only God knows the hearts of believers he has called and that there are some in the visible church who are not genuine believers. The distinction implies that a person must be born again spiritually (having a spiritual birthday) to be in the invisible church. The visible or physical church may have some, like Nicodemus, who are not born again. When referring to "your church," it will be the visible church congregation that you attend. The invisible church will be referred to as "Christ's church." What is your church's role in recognizing and celebrating your spiritual birthday?

THE CHURCH'S SPIRITUAL BIRTHDAY

Most churches and denominations agree that the "church's spiritual birthday" was on the day of Pentecost as recorded in the Acts of the Apostles. Luke's detailed accounts of the origin and growth of the church are fascinating. Can you imagine being there in Jerusalem on the day of Pentecost and attending the launching of Christ's church? Jesus first declared his plans to build his church on earth when God the Father revealed to Peter and the disciples that Jesus was the expected Messiah, or Christ. Jesus said his church would have the keys to the kingdom of heaven and that the gates of hell would not prevail against it. Jesus revealed his heart for the disciples and his future church in the Upper Room Discourse, recorded by John in chapters 14-17 of his Gospel. These teachings and prayers occurred just prior to his betrayal, trial, crucifixion, and resurrection. This was his last teaching to his disciples about what was ahead for him and for them. Jesus was clear on the importance of his returning to the Father and sending the Holy Spirit to be his Advocate for believers and the church. In fact, in John 16:7, Jesus said, *But very truly I tell you, it is for your good that I am going away. Unless I go away, the Advocate will not come to you; but if I go, I will send him to you.* Jesus was limited by his physical humanity. The Holy Spirit reveals all truth that he receives from Jesus. The Spirit is doing the work of God the Father and of Jesus on earth during the church age until Jesus returns for his bride.

Jesus spent forty days on earth after his resurrection appearing to many and speaking about the kingdom of God. Jesus had fulfilled his mission on earth to provide the way of salvation through his death and resurrection. On his last day on earth, Jesus took his disciples to the Mount of Olives outside of Jerusalem to give them final instructions. He reminded them of his earlier promises to build his church and to send the Holy Spirit after going away. He ordered them not to depart from Jerusalem but to wait for the promised Holy Spirit to come in not many days. His last words to them before ascending into a cloud were: *But you will receive power when the Holy Spirit has come upon you, and you will be my witnesses in Jerusalem and all Judea and Samaria, and to the end of the earth* (Acts 1:8).

PENTECOST SUNDAY

Ten days later about 120 believers were together in Jerusalem to celebrate Pentecost, an annual Jewish harvest festival. Suddenly, a sound like a mighty rushing wind filled the entire house where they were sitting. Then, what looked like flames or tongues of fire appeared and settled on each of them. Everyone present was filled with the Holy Spirit and began speaking in other languages as the Holy Spirit gave them ability. Because Pentecost was a pilgrimage festival, Jews from many nations were in Jerusalem and heard the loud noise of the rushing wind, and a crowd came running to the house. When they heard these Galileans speaking in their own native languages about the mighty works of God, they were amazed and perplexed. Some thought the disciples were drunk.

Then Peter, standing with the eleven apostles, lifted up his voice and witnessed to his listeners from Jerusalem, Judea, and the known nations of the Roman and Parthian empires. Many responded to Peter's invitation to repent and receive the Holy Spirit, and about three thousand souls were added that day to the kingdom of God in the name of Jesus Christ—three thousand spiritual birthdays at the first church service!

That would be a megachurch today, but without a building or a budget. Yet they all devoted themselves to the apostles teaching, to fellowship, to sharing meals (including the Lord's Supper), and to prayer. A deep sense of awe came over them all, and the apostles performed many miraculous signs and wonders. All the believers met together in one place and shared everything they had. They sold their property and possessions and shared the money with those in need. They worshiped together at the Temple each day, met in homes for the Lord's Supper, and shared their meals with great joy and generosity, all the while praising God and enjoying the goodwill of all the people. And each day the Lord added to their fellowship those who were being saved. Each saved person was another spiritual birthday to celebrate. Luke's account sounds more like a continuous spiritual birthday celebration than a typical church. Note that the Lord added the new believers to the church. Everyone in Christ's church has a spiritual birthday—and only those who have been born again spiritually through the Holy Spirit are in his church.

THE EARLY CHURCH

The church in Jerusalem continued to grow as more Jews repented and joined the fellowship of believers. The eleven apostles had chosen Matthias to replace Judas, and The Twelve, as they were called, were responsible for the spiritual and physical needs of the fellowship. The Jews from other lands who spoke Greek complained to The Twelve against the Jews who spoke Hebrew about the distribution of food to their widows. The Twelve felt that it would not be right for them to neglect the spiritual ministry to wait tables, so they asked the gathered fellowship to choose seven men full of the Spirit and wisdom to be responsible for the church members' physical needs. These seven men were considered the first deacons and the beginning of the organized church at Jerusalem. The believers in Jerusalem increased rapidly, and many of the Jewish priests became obedient to faith in Jesus as well.

However, the high priest and Jewish leaders, including Saul, were threatened by the rapid growth of Christ's church and initiated a great persecution of the church in Jerusalem, including killing Deacon Stephen. The members of the Jerusalem church scattered throughout Judea and Samaria and were witnesses of Jesus wherever they went.

The early disciples of Christ were referred to as those who belonged to "The Way." They disbursed rapidly to surrounding cities and countries in the Roman Empire. Saul led the attack against The Way and was traveling the 150 miles from Jerusalem to Damascus to imprison them when he suddenly saw a vision from heaven of Jesus speaking to him. His miraculous conversion to faith in Christ was the beginning of Christ's church being taken to the Gentiles, or non-Jewish people, throughout the entire world.

Paul, previously Saul, was the founder of many churches throughout the Roman Empire and the author of many letters to the churches recorded in the New Testament. Antioch, a major Roman city, where Paul spent a year ministering, is where the disciples were first called Christians. Antioch became Paul's home church and the starting point of his three long missionary journeys. His travel, preaching, teachings, and writings, many from Roman prisons, over thirty-three years are hard to imagine, but it has had an unimaginable impact on today's church.

TODAY'S CHURCH

Today's church is still to be Jesus' witness through the Holy Spirit to the ends of the earth. Before your spiritual birthday, the church's role is to introduce you to Jesus and the Holy Spirit who is seeking you. If your parents have spiritual birthdays and therefore are members of Christ's church, this introduction is easier. Your early exposure and introduction to Jesus through your parents and through children's ministries in an organized church laid a good foundation for you to seek Jesus.

As will be discussed in Chapter 7, the church must recognize that children need to make a personal decision to be born again through the Holy Spirit once they have reached the age of accountability. The teaching and spiritual education you receive in church are important to your understanding and desire to be born spiritually. Although many, if not most, spiritual birthdays occur within the organized church facilities, it is important that your church recognize that spiritual birth is through the Holy Spirit and not the church organization. The role of the church is to witness to and lead the spiritual seeker to Christ. The church must realize that the seeker may be a child, a youth, a younger adult, or an older adult with or without a religious background. The church must offer in-house and outreach programs to introduce all ages and backgrounds to the gospel.

CELEBRATING CHURCH MEMBERS

The church has a role at your spiritual birth to celebrate and welcome you into the kingdom of God. Just as the angels in heaven rejoice when one sinner repents and accepts Christ, the church should rejoice and celebrate each new child of God. Just as human families celebrate a physical birth, the church family should celebrate each spiritual birth. Announcing the birth to all church members spreads the joy and celebration.

The role of your church in your spiritual journey should be a lifelong one—including celebrating your spiritual birthdays, spiritual growth, and spiritual achievements. This role is not to be fulfilled primarily by the pastors or staff but by the Christian community that serves and fellowships with you. Your church can promote and help facilitate such celebrations.

SPIRITUAL GROWTH

Like your physical journey after physical birth, the first year after your spiritual birth is very important in your spiritual journey. The Apostle Peter in his first letter to the dispersed Christians in Asia Minor reminds them that God, according to his great mercy, had caused them to be born again to a living hope through the resurrection of Jesus Christ from the dead. (1 Peter 1:3-5). He advises them in 2:2-3, *Like newborn babies, crave pure spiritual milk, so that by it you may grow up in your salvation, now that you have tasted that the Lord is good.* This pure spiritual milk must come primarily through your church and Christian community. The church must recognize the craving for spiritual milk by the newborn believers and provide it gently to change people of the flesh to mature spiritual followers of Christ.

In his writings to the Corinthians and Hebrews, Paul complains that he could not address them as spiritual people but as people of the flesh, as infants in Christ. He fed them with milk, not solid food. Your church can become a nursery of infants in Christ if they are not spiritually fed properly after their spiritual birth.

The role of the organized church to feed and grow God's children to mature members of Christ's church is not without God's help. To each member of Christ's church, the Holy Spirit gives spiritual gifts for the common good of the church. These spiritual gifts vary for each member, but the Spirit appoints the individual gifts required for the entire body. Your organized church must help you to discover your spiritual gift or gifts and how to use them for the common good of the church. Many churches fail in this role and place members in ministry roles different from their spiritual gifts. If you do not know your spiritual gifts, seek help from your church or Christian community.

SPIRITUAL WARFARE

In addition to spiritual gifts to benefit the church, God also provides an armor to protect the church. Paul instructed the church at Ephesus to:

> Put on the whole armor of God, that you may be able to stand against the schemes of the devil. For we do not wrestle against flesh and blood, but against the rulers, against the authorities, against the cosmic powers over this present darkness, against the spiritual forces of evil in the heavenly places. Therefore take up the whole armor of

God, that you may be able to withstand in the evil day,
and having done all, to stand firm (Ephesians 6:11–12
ESV).

This warning is for the corporate body and for the individual members of the church. Your church must equip you with the whole armor of God. They must provide the belt of truth, the breastplate of righteousness, and the shoes of readiness given by the gospel of peace. You must have the shield of faith, the helmet of salvation and the sword of the Spirit, which is the Word of God, to fight against the evil one. The organized church is your whole armor of God equipment manager and armor bearer to help you stand firm and win the spiritual warfare that you face on your spiritual journey.

SHARING THE GOSPEL

Your church should also provide instruction and resources to help you share your spiritual birthday story and to share the gospel story. Your story may lead your family and friends, who do not know Jesus as their savior, to repentance and to their own spiritual birth through the Holy Spirit. Often, new born-again believers are the most excited and anxious to share their joy and their spiritual birthday story, for they realize the need everyone has for a spiritual birth. Older Christians can share the changes in their lives and the results of knowing and serving Christ. The spiritual stories being lived today are as inspiring and often as miraculous as stories recorded in Scripture. The Holy Spirit is still working today as he did in Bible days.

The reality and relativity of today's stories have lessons and examples to reach unbelievers and teach believers. Many pastors are missing opportunities to include current stories of spiritual births and testimonies of members in their teachings. The organized church needs to focus on evangelism to those without a spiritual birthday. You need your church's leadership and support to reach those outside of Christ's church with the gospel story.

HEAVEN

Your church has an important role to promote the big celebration of eternal life in heaven reserved only for those with spiritual birthdays. Your spiritual journey has a destination that is beyond your imagination. God has revealed a glimpse of heaven by his Spirit, but it is still difficult for us to imagine eternal life with Jesus in heaven. The organized church must focus members on their destination so that they will desire to see and enter the kingdom of God. Jesus explained to Nicodemus that he alone had come from heaven and told him twice that no one can see or enter the kingdom of God without being born again. Celebrating heaven as our destination should not be reserved only for funeral services but should be promoted in church services and outreach events.

CELEBRATING PENTECOST SUNDAY

The church celebrates Christmas to remember that God so loved the world that he gave his one and only Son. It celebrates Easter Sunday to remember that Jesus so loved the world that he suffered and died and rose again so that whoever believes in him shall not perish but have eternal life. These are big celebrations in the church. The church also needs to celebrate Pentecost Sunday to remember that God sent the Holy Spirit to carry out Jesus' promise to build his church.

Pentecost Sunday marks the dividing line between the ministry of the Lord and the ministry of the Spirit. It is the birth of the Christian church as an institution. In the Old Testament, God instructed his people to celebrate. After he freed the Israelites, his chosen people, from their bondage in Egypt, he instructed Moses to celebrate three annual feasts, God gave the date, length, and activity of each celebration to Moses in great detail as part of the Law. The Jewish Law, including the Ten Commandments, was given to Moses at Mount Sinai fifty days after the exodus from Egypt. The three feasts were the Feast of Unleavened Bread, the Feast of Weeks, and the Feast of Tabernacles. The Feast of Unleavened Bread began the day after the Passover. The Feast of Weeks, also known as the Harvest Celebration, was to be celebrated seven weeks after the Feast of Unleavened Bread or fifty days after the Passover. Since Pentecost means fifty, the date of the Feast of Weeks became known as Pentecost.

Celebrating Pentecost Sunday today by the Christian church is not a continuation of the Old Testament Jewish Feast of Weeks. Pentecost took on a new and more significant meaning in the New Testament. Fifty days after Easter Sunday, when Jesus' resurrection freed us from the bondage of sin, God sent the Holy Spirit to testify of Jesus as the fulfillment of the Law. The New Testament Pentecost Sunday is a new harvest of souls celebration.

All Christian churches should celebrate Pentecost Sunday as the coming of the Holy Spirit in a new role. The Holy Spirit is building Christ's church one spiritual birth at a time. He is working in countless ways in the spiritual life of churches and individuals. He dwells in those with a spiritual birthday and is ever present, as Jesus promised.

Celebrating Pentecost Sunday is not about speaking in tongues but about Spirit-filled Galilean apostles speaking the gospel message to men from every nation on earth in their native language. Pentecost Sunday is about the diversity included in the Great Commission given by Jesus just before he ascended into heaven.

Pentecost Sunday is about the close bond between the church and the Holy Spirit. We need Spirit-filled churches filled with Spirit-filled people. The Holy Spirit, often the forgotten person of God, must be celebrated for the work he is doing through born-again believers sharing the gospel story. Just as Jesus was bringing glory to God, the Father, the Spirit is bringing glory to Jesus the Son.

Millions of born-again Christians, all remembering and celebrating their spiritual birth on Pentecost Sunday, would be a very big celebration on earth like there will be in heaven. The organized church is missing an opportunity to celebrate the continuing work of the Holy Spirit and the church that Jesus is still building. If Pentecost Sunday is considered too Old Testament or has negative connotations in your church, rename it "Spiritual Birthday Sunday" and celebrate. Celebrating the Spirit and the church would be a unique and powerful Christian celebration of the kingdom of God on earth.

Unlike Christmas and Easter, where secular society has added Santa Claus and "Happy Holidays" or bunnies and colored eggs to Christian holidays, there are no such social markers for Pentecost Sunday. Whether your church recognizes and celebrates Pentecost Sunday seven Sundays after Easter or not, you can personally celebrate the Holy Spirit that came to give you spiritual birth and resides within you after your spiritual birthday.

LIVING STONES

Many churches are built with a cornerstone that anchors and establishes the building construction. Jesus is the cornerstone of our faith. I like the image of the church described in 1 Peter 2:4-6:

> *As you come to him, the living Stone rejected by men but chosen by God and precious to him; you also, like living stones, are being built into a spiritual house to be a holy priesthood, offering spiritual sacrifices acceptable to God through Jesus Christ. For in Scriptures it says, "See I lay a stone in Zion, a chosen and precious cornerstone, and the one who trusts in him will never be put to shame."*

Peter was writing to those who had been born again, those with a spiritual birthday. God is building his spiritual temple with Christ as the cornerstone, and all with spiritual birthdays as living stones. Celebrate that you are a living stone in the invisible church that Christ is building.

CHAPTER 7

LITTLE CHILDREN

At that time, Jesus, full of joy through the Holy Spirit, said,
"I praise you, Father, Lord of heaven and earth,
because you have hidden these things from the wise and
learned, and revealed them to the little children.
Yes, Father, for this was your good pleasure."

Luke 10:21

Can you remember being a little child? Your childhood was a very special and unique period in your life. You may have seen photographs or videos to help you remember your early years and activities. Can you recall your imagination as you played with stuffed animals, dolls, toys, balls, games, and friends? As a child, you imagined and dreamed of what you wanted to become as an adult. As an adult, can you imagine becoming like a little child again?

During Jesus' ministry, people were bringing little children to Jesus for him to put his hand on them, but the disciples rebuked them. Luke's account says,

> *When Jesus saw this, he was indignant. He said to them,*
> *"Let the little children come to me, and do not hinder*
> *them, for the kingdom of God belongs to such as these.*
> *I tell you the truth, anyone who will not receive the*
> *kingdom of God like a little child will never enter it."*
> **(Luke 18:16-17)**

And he took the children in his arms, placed his hand on them, and blessed them.

This account, recorded in all three synoptic gospels, has similarities to John's gospel account of Jesus's conversation with Nicodemus regarding entering the kingdom of God. Jesus emphasized both teachings: "Truly, I tell you," he told Nicodemus, "You must be born again to enter the kingdom of God." He told the disciples, "You must receive the kingdom of God like a little child to enter it." Can you imagine becoming like a little child and receiving the kingdom of God? Being born again and becoming like a little child are both counter to our adult experience. Yet, spiritually, you must be born of the Spirit and become like an innocent and believing child as you accept God's gift of Jesus to enter the kingdom of God.

WHO IS GREATEST IN HEAVEN?

On another occasion, the disciples came to Jesus and asked, *Who, then, is the greatest in the kingdom of heaven?* Jesus called a child, whom he placed before them. And he said,

> *I tell you the truth, unless you change and become like*
> *little children, you will never enter the kingdom of heaven.*

Therefore, whoever humbles himself like this child is the greatest in the kingdom of heaven. And whoever welcomes a child like this in my name welcomes me.
(Matthew 18:2–5)

Jesus knew that the disciples argued over who was the greatest and who would sit at his right and left hand in heaven. These men, who had heard his teachings for years and were his closest friends, needed to become like little children to enter the kingdom of heaven. Nicodemus, a Jewish religious leader and teacher, needed to be born again to enter the kingdom of heaven. Jesus used a little child not only to teach how to enter the kingdom of heaven but also to indicate who is greatest in the kingdom of heaven. Born-again believers are referred to in Scripture as children of God. Being a child of God and entering the kingdom of God are mysterious realities that Jesus taught through his life and ministry. It is important to remember that children of God are not born of natural descent, nor of human decision, nor of a husband's will, but born of God.

Can you imagine God condemning innocent little children to an eternity in hell because of the sin of Adam or their parents? The Bible teaches that we all have inherited the sinful nature of our human ancestors, Adam and Eve, who committed the original sin of disobedience by eating fruit from the tree of the knowledge of good and evil. The nature of the sin may have significance as it relates to little children. They ate from the forbidden tree, the tree of the knowledge of good and evil. The words "knowledge of" may have significance.

ADAM AND EVE LIKE LITTLE CHILDREN?

Can you imagine Adam and Eve being created like innocent little children? Can you imagine them like little children as God brought all the animals and birds to Adam, and his new playmate Eve, to name? It required a childlike imagination to name all living creatures. Can you imagine them like little children running around naked in the Garden of Eden, but feeling no shame? God treated Adam like a little child and gave him only one "Must Not." In the garden, God had planted all kinds of trees that were pleasing to the eye and good for food. But in the middle of the garden were the tree of life and the tree of the knowledge of good and evil. God commanded Adam, *You are free to eat from any tree in the garden; but you must not eat from the tree of the knowledge of good and evil, for when you eat of it you will surely die* (Genesis 2:16-17).

Adam, apparently like a child, did not question God's instructions and ate only fruit from other trees as he was naming animals and getting acquainted with his playmate Eve. He told her about the one rule that God had given him regarding the trees and she, like a child, did not question why they should not eat from the tree in the middle of the garden.

Then God allowed Satan, a fallen and evil angel, to cause Eve to question God's command.

> *Satan questioned Eve saying, "Did God really say, 'You must not eat from any tree in the garden'?"*

Eve innocently replied, "We may eat fruit from the trees in the garden, but God did say, 'You must not eat fruit from the tree that is in the middle of the garden, and you must not touch it, or you will die.'"

Satan then tempts her by saying, "You will not surely die. For God knows that when you eat of it your eyes will be opened, and you will be like God, knowing good and evil."

When Eve saw that the fruit of the tree was good for food and pleasing to the eye (like all the other trees), but also desirable for gaining wisdom, she took some and ate it. She also gave some to her husband, who was with her, and he ate it. **(Genesis 3:1-6)**

You know the rest of the story. Adam and Eve immediately realized that they were naked, and they hid from God. God held the serpent as well as Eve and Adam accountable for breaking his one commandment.

LITTLE CHILDREN IN THE OLD TESTAMENT

Do little children have a God-given grace that guarantees them heaven before they reach the age of accountability? We need to look further in Scripture for God's treatment of little children. In the Old Testament account of the Israelites' journey from captivity in Egypt to the Promised Land, the people were concerned about their children being taken captive. The people did not trust God's promises to go with them, and they refused to go into the new land.

God's punishment was that the Israelites would wander forty more years in the wilderness and the adults would not go into the promised land. Forty years later, Moses spoke to Israel about what God had said regarding their rebellion. God said, *And the little ones that you said would be taken captive, your children who do not yet know good from bad—they will enter the land. I will give it to them and they will take possession of it* (Deuteronomy 1:39). The promised land was symbolic of heaven. It appears in Scripture that there is a point when a child has the knowledge or ability to choose right from wrong and to accept or reject the gospel. This is often referred to as the "age of accountability" or "the age of reason," though the church has struggled with the question of when this age of accountability occurs.

David committed adultery with Bathsheba, the wife of Uriah, and she conceived a son. Then David had Uriah killed to hide his sexual sin. So God sent Nathan the prophet to confront David about his sin and warn him of God's anger. David confessed his sin against the Lord. Nathan replied, *The Lord has taken away your sin. You are not going to die. But because by doing this you have made the enemies of the Lord show utter contempt, the son born to you will die* (2 Samuel 12:13-14). The child became ill and David pleaded with God to spare his son. On the seventh day, the child died and David's attendants were afraid to tell him. They were surprised when David stopped grieving once the boy died. David answered, *While the child was still alive, I fasted and wept. I thought, "Who knows? The Lord may be gracious to me and let the child live." But now that he is dead, why should I fast? Can I bring him back again? I will go to him, but he will not return to me"* (2

Samuel 12:22-23). Many interpret this to mean David had hope and faith that he would see his little child again.

JESUS AS A CHILD

Luke the physician is the only gospel writer who discusses the dedication of Jesus in the temple in Jerusalem when he was forty days old. Joseph and Mary took him to Jerusalem as an infant to be consecrated to the Lord and to offer a sacrifice as required by the Law of the Lord. They returned home to Nazareth, and Luke writes, *And the child grew and became strong; he was filled with wisdom and the grace of God was on him* (Luke 2:40). Luke then relates the story of Joseph and Mary's annual trip to Jerusalem when Jesus was twelve years old to celebrate the Feast of the Passover. Everything went as usual for the family during the celebration, but after a day of travel home toward Nazareth, Jesus was missing from the company of family and friends. It took them more than three days to find Jesus in the temple courts sitting with the rabbis, listening and asking questions of these teachers. Everyone who heard Jesus was amazed at his understanding and his answers. His earthly parents were both astonished and angry with him for making them search for him in great distress. Jesus asked, *Why were you searching for me? Didn't you know that I had to be in my Father's house?* (Luke 2:49).

Luke closes the story of the twelve-year-old Jesus by relating that he went down to Nazareth with them (Joseph and Mary) and was obedient to them. *And as Jesus grew up, he increased in wisdom and in favor with God and people* (Luke 2:52). Note the difference between Luke's two descriptions of Jesus' growth. As a little child, the grace of God was on him. As a young adult, he increased in favor with God. It seems that Jesus had reached the age of accountability. He was now accountable for his increase in favor with God.

GOD LOVES LITTLE CHILDREN

God's love for little children and their special grace and place in his kingdom is important for parents and the church to understand. The desire of Christian parents and grandparents is for their young children or grandchildren to have faith in Jesus and have eternal life in heaven. God's desire is for all children to believe and have saving faith in Jesus once they reach an age of accountability. Understanding and believing God's provision and plan for little children allows you to focus on your response and responsibility as a parent or church. Your responsibility is to *Train a child in the way he should go, and when he is old he will not turn from it* (Proverbs 22.6).

Paul wrote to the Ephesians, *Fathers, do not exasperate your children; bring them up in the training and instruction of the Lord* (Ephesians 6:4). A Christian parent is to prepare and nurture the spiritual birth of the child. Remember that neither you nor the church can give spiritual birth to God's children. It is a gift through Jesus and the Holy Spirit. The timeline for a physical birth is approximately nine months. The timeline for a spiritual birthday may extend much beyond the age of accountability. As a parent or grandparent, you can only pray for a spiritual birthday early in your child's physical life. Jesus encouraged parents to bring their babies and little children to him and warned his disciples not to turn them away. If little children come to know about Jesus and his love early in life, they are more likely to follow him when they reach the age when they really understand good and evil.

BABY DEDICATION

Christian parents should dedicate or commit their children to God as early as possible. As soon as Mary had fulfilled the forty-day purification period required before she could enter the temple, she and Joseph dedicated Jesus to God. Hopefully, your church encourages baby dedication and commits to helping parents bring their children to faith in Jesus at an early age. As parents, you are committing to plant the seeds and encourage the spiritual birth of your child just as you nurture their physical and mental growth. To publicly dedicate your young child to God in front of family and the church congregation confirms your desire to raise your children in a God-centered home and bring them to faith in Jesus.

Many Christian churches follow a tradition of baptizing infants to symbolize that their parents, and often godparents, are dedicating their child to God. This is generally a sincere commitment to raise and train the child in a godly manner and bring them to a personal faith in Jesus. These same churches usually recognize that the child, upon reaching the age of accountability, must personally affirm his or her faith in Jesus. Confirmation must be an inward working of the Holy Spirit in each individual as they understand their need for a savior and choose to follow Jesus.

THE ROLE OF PARENTS AND THE CHURCH

Christian parents of little children have an important role in the spiritual journey of each child. The formative years before a child reaches the age of accountability are when you must lay the spiritual foundation to build upon. Mothers and fathers can input spiritual truth to their children while they are infants. Children learn to understand their parents' feelings and emotions before they even learn to talk. Your tone of voice, affection, and time spent with them are early indicators of your love.

Music and Bible stories can introduce small children to God. Prayer at meals, bedtime, and family devotions exposes children to Jesus on a daily basis and teaches them that he is our provider and friend. The years prior to entering school are good ones to impart basic Christian truths and activities. While many television programs do not offer positive role models for children, there are many Christian videos and resources available to teach Bible stories and Christian values on a child's level. It is never too early to begin the process of helping your children develop biblical beliefs.

Partner with your church in the spiritual development of your child. The church can play a significant role in helping parents bring their children to faith in Jesus. The church should be a support community by providing spiritual insight to equip and encourage parents. Many churches provide active and exciting programs for children during their adult worship services. Experienced and trained teachers using well-designed curriculum can provide spiritual instruction and help to bring your child to a saving knowledge of Jesus. Show interest and take part in your child's church activities and programs. An involved parent is best able to nurture the spiritual development of his or her child.

Physical, emotional, intellectual, and spiritual development in children is a fairly predictable process. Yet each child is unique and develops at his or her own pace. Just as the physical environment impacts their physical development, their spiritual environment influences their spiritual development. A child growing up in an active Christian family that is living and practicing their faith will likely develop their own understanding and faith at an earlier age than a child without that example. Do not pressure children to make an early decision to follow Jesus, but don't discourage it either! Allow the Holy Spirit to work and call them to faith on his timeline.

If you believe that they understand the gospel message and are ready to make a personal commitment to trust Jesus as their Savior, try to lead them in doing so. When they do, rejoice and celebrate their spiritual birthday. Let them know that the angels in heaven are rejoicing because they have found Jesus. Continue to celebrate and remind them of the significance of their decision. For new believers who are young, consider remembering and celebrating the monthly anniversary of their spiritual birthday during the first year so they realize how important the date is in their lives. Be sure to record the date and help them tell their story to family and friends. New believers need encouragement and help growing in their spiritual walk with Jesus. The Holy Spirit will help them further understand the gospel message and its power in living for Jesus. Parents and the church must continue to nurture and train these newer believers in their spiritual growth—which is a journey that continues for eternity.

UNBORN CHILDREN

Many parents have experienced miscarriages during the mother's pregnancy and have never known or held their child. God's creation of a spiritual being is eternal and precious to him both before and after physical birth. The death of a fetus in the womb is under his grace. I'm convinced, for reasons I explained earlier, that it receives eternal life in the kingdom of God. Because of this, I believe that millions of aborted babies' souls will be in heaven. Not as little winged angels flying around heaven, but as spiritual beings that have entered God's promised land without wandering in the wilderness of this world. In Ecclesiastes 4:2-3, Solomon expressed his observations: *"And I declared that the dead, who have already died, are happier than the living, who are still alive. But better than both is he who has not been, who has not seen the evil that is done under the sun."* If you are a woman who aborted your child, I believe you may meet them in heaven if you repent and put your trust in Jesus as your Forgiver and Savior. I think your soul will recognize their soul. In the same vein, I'm convinced that siblings and relatives of deceased children can also look forward to meeting or reuniting with their family in heaven.

The spiritual birthday of these innocent born or unborn children, whose physical life ended before they reached the age of accountability, can be celebrated on the date their spirit departed their physical body. Rather than mourn the death of their physical body each year, celebrate the spiritual birthday they are now experiencing in heaven. As indicated earlier, I have a brother, twin brothers, and a sister who died at birth, who I have never known on earth but look forward to meeting in heaven. I am reminded of their individual physical birth and death dates each year as I decorate their graves and try to imagine what their physical appearance and earthly journey would have been over the many years if they had lived. I now celebrate their death date as their spiritual birthday and try to imagine their spiritual journey in heaven.

BE THERE FOR LITTLE CHILDREN

Jesus loves the little children of this world; the kingdom of God belongs to them and to those who become like little children. Be there for little children on earth and do not hinder them as they come to Jesus.

One concern may be that young children may want to have a spiritual birthday to celebrate like older family members before they understand good and evil and the significance of a spiritual birth. Only the Spirit can know their heart and understanding. He can eventually bring transformation and give spiritual birth. This childlike desire is your opportunity to share God's plan of salvation and the meaning of spiritual birth in terms they can understand. You may share your story of being born again at an older age. It was difficult for Nicodemus to understand and might be for your young child as well.

Celebrating your spiritual birthday with little children is an opportunity to share your story of coming to a saving faith in Jesus and its significance in your life since that day. Bringing little children to Jesus and helping them understand his love for them is vitally important in their spiritual journey.

CHAPTER 8

THE BIG CELEBRATION

After this I looked, and there before me was a great multitude
that no one could count, from every nation, tribe, people
and language, standing before the throne and in front of the
Lamb. They were wearing white robes and were holding
palm branches in their hands.

Revelation 8:9

Can you imagine the world without celebrations? Can you imagine not celebrating Christmas and the New Year? During your earthly journey, you have seen or experienced huge celebrations. Human beings all over the world love to celebrate.

New Year's Day is celebrated all around the world. Christmas and Easter are big celebrations for Christian nations. More than two billion people celebrate Jesus' birthday each year. Many celebrate Christmas with unusual traditions that seem to have little spiritual significance. Christmas has become a big celebration for retailers as they promote gifts, cards, decorations, food, and travel. Retail sales in the United States alone exceed $600 billion dollars—averaging over $800 per shopper.

It is important for Jesus' followers to remember the real reason for the season. It is a time to celebrate Jesus' physical birth as he came to earth as our Savior. On the night Jesus was born, the angels told the shepherds that they brought good news of great joy for all people, because a savior had been born in the town of David. He was Christ the Lord. Christmas is a good time to celebrate your spiritual birthday, remembering that Jesus was born so you may be born again. It is good news of great joy that should cause you to rejoice and celebrate.

LIFE'S BIG CELEBRATIONS

On a more personal basis, you likely have experienced big celebrations during your life's journey. Weddings are often big family celebrations with relatives and friends joining the bride and groom with gifts, flowers, food, music, and dancing in a beautifully decorated setting. Big celebrations are exciting to imagine and plan and are usually only limited by your finances. The weeks of planning and anticipation preceding a big celebration are often more exciting and memorable than the event itself, which only lasts a few hours. However, the thrill and experience of being together with family and friends for a special event is good, even if only for a few hours. Hopefully, you have experienced many big celebrations—including family birthdays, weddings, and family reunions.

YOUR DESTINATION?

Often, we become so focused on day-to-day living that we forget our destination. Our physical journey on earth has a destination that many do not want to consider, let alone celebrate. God said to Adam in response to his disobedience, *By the sweat of your brow you will eat your food until you return to the ground, since from it you were taken; for dust you are and to dust you will return* (Genesis 3:19). Your physical body's destination is the grave. Medical science may prolong your journey, but you will still arrive at the same destination. The psalmist wrote: *The years of our life are seventy, or even by reason of strength eighty; yet their span is but toil and trouble; they are soon gone, and we fly away* (Psalm 90:10). You may reach your physical destination much earlier than expected through accident or illness.

Your journey's destination can be a big celebration if you have planned your spiritual journey well. Many plan for their family's future physical well-being through insurance, trusts, and physical assets but neglect to plan for their own spiritual well-being. When your body (your physical being) reaches its destination (the grave), your soul (your spiritual being) leaves your body and goes to its destination. Your soul's destination on its spiritual journey will be heaven or hell, depending on which plan you chose during your physical journey.

God's preferred plan, which was paid for by Jesus, is for you to be with him in heaven for eternity. Can you imagine that Jesus went to prepare a place for you and when it is ready, he will come for you so you may be where he is? Satan's plan is for you to be with him and his fallen angels in hell. Can you imagine the thirst and torment described by Jesus in his parable in Luke's gospel (Luke 16) and by John in the Book of Revelation? Your choice will determine the destination where your soul will spend eternity. The saying: "Born Once, Die Twice; Born Twice, Die Once" confirms "You must be born again."

HEAVEN'S BIG CELEBRATION

Scripture makes it very clear that heaven will be a celebration bigger than any celebration experienced on earth. The glory and splendor of heaven are beyond human imagination, comprehension, or description. It will be "The Big Celebration." Paul quoted the Old Testament prophet Isaiah, saying, *No eye has seen, no ear has heard, no mind has conceived what God has prepared for those who love him.* But Paul goes on to say, *But God has revealed it to us by his Spirit* (1 Corinthians 2:9-10).

Paul later describes being caught up to heaven, where he heard inexpressible things that man is not permitted to tell. The Apostle John writes in the book of Revelation a detailed account of his vision of heaven. He reports seeing and hearing 100,000,000 angels singing together in a loud voice with every creature in heaven and on earth. He witnessed a great multitude that no one could count, from every nation, tribe, people, and language, standing before the throne waving branches and shouting in a loud voice. He saw flashes of lightning, an earthquake, and a hailstorm. He heard thunder, trumpets, and harps. He smelled incense. John certainly was trying to describe a big celebration. He also noted what he did not see. No more death or mourning or crying or pain. The celebration was on streets of gold, and there was no night. Jesus and his glory are the focus of heaven. John's brief glimpse of heaven is only a snapshot of an eternal celebration. It is like a small ad for a beautiful and glorious destination with great accommodations and an eternal stay.

All big celebrations on earth have an ending. The birthday party is over and your guests have gone home. Only the photos and memories remain. The wedding, the reception, and the wedding dance are over, and the bride and groom have left on their honeymoon. The reunion is over, and you must say goodbye until next time. Christmas is over, and you must take down the tree and decorations. You may have to return and exchange unwanted or wrong-sized gifts. John could have added many "No Mores" to the list; like an end to the celebrations.

CELEBRATING FOREVER

Heaven, however, is a *forever* celebration. Can you imagine your excitement when Jesus reads your name from his Lamb's Book of Life? Millions of angels and saints of God will cheer and celebrate with you. Can you imagine the celebration in heaven when Jesus casts Satan into the lake of fire and there is no more evil? God will create a new heaven and a new earth for the celebration. Jesus will come back with his bride, the church, and reign forever.

John heard a loud voice from the throne saying,

> *Now the dwelling of God is with men, and he will live with them. They will be his people and God himself will be with them and be their God. He will wipe every tear from their eyes. There will be no more death or mourning or crying or pain, for the old order of things has passed away. He who was seated on the throne said, "I am making all things new! Write this down, for these words are trustworthy and true."* **(Revelation 21:3-5)**

You can trust these promises from Jesus, who was sitting on the throne in heaven, to be true. John wrote down his words for you. So be sure to *Be There*! *Be There* at The Big Celebration. Determine now to *Be There*. Above every other purpose and goal on your physical journey, the only thing that really matters is that you *Be There* and that you bring as many friends and loved ones with you as possible.

Your spiritual birthday represents your decision and determination to *Be There* to celebrate with Jesus.

CELEBRATE

I wrote this book not about my spiritual birthday, or about me, but about you having and celebrating your spiritual birthday. My prayer is for you to be born again and enter the kingdom of God. Your soul seeks God. The Holy Spirit seeks your soul. Your spiritual birthday is when you find each other in a personal encounter and you are born again. You are born of the Spirit and become a child of God. You enter the kingdom of God. Your soul is saved and secured by the Spirit from the One who can kill the soul. Understanding this truth and being born spiritually is my reason for writing *Your Spiritual Birthday.*

My purpose is to encourage you to celebrate your spiritual birthday annually to highlight, strengthen, and proclaim your spiritual life and journey with Jesus. Celebrating is an expression of your love for God and a witness to the world. Because the church has generally not recorded or celebrated spiritual birthdays, you may not know the actual date you were born again, so my advice is "Pick a Date and Celebrate."

CELEBRATE YOUR SPIRITUAL BIRTHDAY

Celebrate your spiritual birthday in a way that reflects your love for God and your joy of being his child. Rejoice that your name is written in Jesus' Book of Life. Celebrate your new life in Christ. Celebrate your victory over death. You have won. You have entered the Kingdom of God. Share your celebration with your brothers and sisters in Christ. Your spiritual birthday celebration should exceed all other celebrations. Your spiritual birth was the most important event in your life, so become a contagiously celebratory Christian!

CELEBRATE YOUR PHYSICAL BIRTHDAY

Celebrate your physical birthday with a new appreciation for being miraculously created by God for a physical and spiritual purpose. Celebrate that you can worship and serve God with your physical strength and ask him to keep you strong and holy. Paul wrote to the church in Rome, *Therefore, I urge you, brothers, in view of God's mercy, to offer your bodies as a living sacrifice, holy and pleasing to God; this is your spiritual act of worship* (Romans 12:1). Celebrate that your body is a temple of the Holy Spirit, whom you have received from God. You are not your own. Celebrating your physical birthday with family and friends may give opportunities to share that you also have and celebrate a spiritual birthday as well.

CELEBRATE JESUS' BIRTHDAY

Celebrate Jesus' birthday. Your spiritual birthday gives you more reason to celebrate the Christmas season. Jesus is the reason you have a spiritual birthday to celebrate. Celebrate God the Father for the amazing gift he gave you on the first Christmas. Celebrate Jesus, *"Who being in the very nature God, did not consider equality with God something to be grasped, but made himself nothing, taking the very nature of a servant, being made in human likeness"* (Philippians 2:6-7). Celebrate as the angels did that first Christmas night by giving glory to God in the highest.

CELEBRATE YOUR SPIRITUAL JOURNEY

Celebrate your spiritual journey on earth and your new life in Christ. Celebrate your believer's baptism to proclaim your saving faith in Christ and to symbolize your spiritual baptism by the Holy Spirit. Celebrate your spiritual gifts by serving your church family and others outside the church. Prepare yourself for spiritual warfare by putting on the whole armor of God, so you may stand against the forces of evil and standing firm, celebrate your victory through the Spirit.

CELEBRATE JESUS' JOURNEY

Celebrate Jesus' earthly journey and teachings by studying Scripture. Celebrate Easter, remembering that Jesus' journey on earth ended with suffering and physical death, providing the way for your sins to be forgiven and for you to have a spiritual birthday. Celebrate Jesus' victory over death and that through his resurrection, he gives you victory over sin and spiritual death. Celebrate the hope you have in Christ for eternal life in heaven through his resurrection.

CELEBRATE LITTLE CHILDREN

Celebrate little children for their innocence, childlike faith, and trust in Jesus. Recognize their special grace from God before they reach the age of accountability or have knowledge of good and evil. Do not hinder them from coming to Jesus or cause these little ones who believe in Jesus to stumble. Plant the seed of God's love in their hearts and continue to cultivate and water the seed. Celebrate when they understand good and evil and accept Jesus as their Savior and Lord.

CELEBRATE PENTECOST SUNDAY

Celebrate Pentecost Sunday, the day that the Holy Spirit came as Jesus had promised. Celebrate the spiritual birthday of the church as the disciples were filled with the Holy Spirit and told of the mighty works of God. Celebrate the spiritual birth of the three thousand who heard the message in their own language and believed and were baptized that day. Celebrate the Holy Spirit for coming to be your advocate and giving you spiritual birth.

CELEBRATE YOUR LOCAL CHURCH

Celebrate your church and the important role it has in your spiritual journey and life. Celebrate your fellowship with other born-again believers as you worship and serve Jesus together. Celebrate and use your spiritual gifts for the common good of your church. Join in celebrating new spiritual births within the church family and the spiritual birthdays of all your brothers and sisters in Christ.

CELEBRATE OTHER'S SPIRITUAL BIRTHDAYS

Celebrate and rejoice with the angels in heaven over every sinner who repents and is saved. In the parable of the prodigal son, the father said, *But we had to celebrate and be glad because this brother of yours was dead and is alive again; he was lost and is found.* Celebrate each new spiritual birthday with wholehearted thanks to Jesus.

BE THERE FOR THE BIG CELEBRATION

Celebrate that you will *Be There* in heaven at the Big Celebration. Determine now to *be there.* Imagine the Big Celebration at the end of your physical life's journey as you enter the kingdom of heaven and experience eternal life with him. You can only imagine the place Jesus went to prepare for you and his glory that he wants you to see when you are with him in heaven.

CELEBRATE TOGETHER FOREVER

Thank you for allowing me to imagine with you and to write about your spiritual birthday. I hope to meet you someday. If not on this side of heaven, look for me in that eternal city. "After you have been there ten thousand years, a million, maybe two, look for me, for I will *be there* too" (Rusty Goodman song).

We will celebrate together forever.

MY SPIRITUAL
BIRTHDAY LIST

Name	Date
_____	_____
_____	_____
_____	_____
_____	_____
_____	_____
_____	_____
_____	_____
_____	_____
_____	_____
_____	_____
_____	_____
_____	_____

RESOURCES

FOR FURTHER READING:

The Case for Christ, Lee Strobel (Zondervan 1998).

Becoming a Contagious Christian, Bill Hybels & Mark Mittelberg (Zondervan 1994).

The Holy Spirit Book, Roy Lessin (Art Set Apart 2017).

The Unexpected Adventure, Lee Strobel & Mark Mittelberg (Zondervan 2009).

Heaven, Randy Alcorn (Tyndale 2004).

The Reason Why Faith Makes Sense, Mark Mittelberg (Tyndale 2011).

The Holy Spirit: Activating God's Power in Your Life, Billy Graham (Thomas Nelson 2000)

Forgotten God: Reversing Our Tragic Neglect of the Holy Spirit, Francis Chan (David C. Cook 2009)

FOR ONLINE RESEARCH:

www.AllAboutGod.com.
www.SpiritualBirthday.com
http://www.Resources.ChurchLeaders.com
www.SermonCentral.com
www.OutreachMagazine.com

THE SPIRITUAL BIRTHDAY SONG

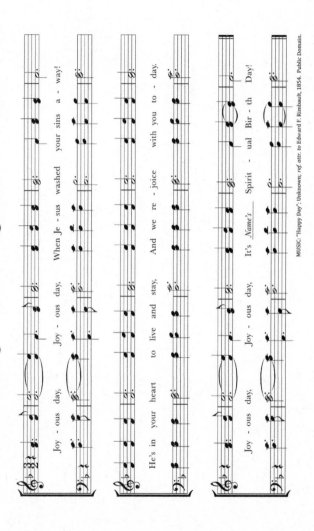

Joy - ous day; Joy - ous day; When Je - sus washed your sins a - way!

He's in your heart to live and stay, And we re - joice with you to - day.

Joy - ous day; Joy - ous day; It's _Name's_ Spirit - ual Bir - th Day!

MUSIC: "Happy Day"; *ref. attr. to* Edward F. Rimbault, 1854. Public Domain.

SPIRITUAL BIRTH
CERTIFICATE

I imagine you have seen your physical birth certificate. It is a vital record that documents your birth. It is the responsibility of the attending physician, hospital administrator, midwife, or parents to certify the time, date, and circumstances of your birth and to see that it is properly registered with the appropriate government jurisdiction. The government's registrar will sign, seal, retain, and store your original birth certificate. Your birth registration secures your rights to preserve your identity, including nationality, name, and family relations. It also certifies information required by governmental or private agencies to prove your age, to prove your nationality, receive healthcare, go to school, take exams, be adopted, marry, open bank accounts, drive, get a passport, inherit money or property, vote, hold an elected office, and have protection from underage military service or juvenile abuse. It is a small paper but establishes who you are and gives you access to the rights, privileges, and obligations of citizenship.

Your *spiritual* birth is recorded in the Lamb's Book of Life according to Scripture. Jesus Christ was first referred to as the Lamb of God by John the Baptist (John 1: 29) and reaffirmed the next day in the presence of the first two disciples to follow Jesus. Unlike your physical birth, which was visible and could be certified by others, your spiritual birth is invisible and can only be certified by the Holy Spirit. Flesh gives birth to flesh, but the Spirit gives birth to spirit. The Spirit certifies and seals your decision to repent of your sins and accept Christ as your personal savior. Jesus registers your spiritual birth in his Book of Life in heaven, which guarantees your eternal life as a child of God and as a citizen of the kingdom of God. As a child of God, you are an adopted son or daughter. You are an heir of God and a co-heir with Christ. You have access to the rights, benefits, privileges, and obligations of citizenship in the kingdom of The King of kings. Your obligation is to love the Lord with all your heart and with all your soul and with all your mind.

Your local church may give certificates for baby dedications, infant baptisms, believer's baptisms, and confirmations. These certify physical acts or sacraments of the church. The Spirit himself testifies with your spirit that you are God's child. The Spirit gives birth to spirit. You are born again. You are born of the Spirit. Only you, through your spirit, can certify that you are born spiritually. Your repentance for your sins and your saving faith in Jesus as your personal Savior and Lord can only be claimed and proclaimed by you. Your love for the Lord, your love for your neighbor, and your good works will confirm your spiritual faith and birth.

You may desire a spiritual birth certificate as a physical representation of your spiritual birth recorded in the Lamb's Book of Life in heaven. Your spiritual birth certificate must be prepared and certified by you personally, testifying that you believe and receive Jesus for eternal salvation. You may use or adapt the following spiritual birth certificate format to document your spiritual birthday.

SPIRITUAL BIRTH CERTIFICATE

WHEREAS all have sinned and fall short of the glory of God (Romans 3:23), and

WHEREAS God shows his love for us in that while we were still sinners, Christ died for us (Romans 5:8), and

WHEREAS the wages of sin is death, but the gift of God is eternal life in Jesus Christ our Lord (Romans 6:23), and

WHEREAS if you confess with your mouth the Lord Jesus and believe in your heart that God has raised him from the dead, you will be saved (Romans 10:9), and

WHEREAS I confessed that I have sinned against God and his Commandments, and

WHEREAS I repented of my sins and turned to God for forgiveness, and

WHEREAS I believed in my heart that Jesus died for my sins and was resurrected for my salvation, and

WHEREAS I received Jesus Christ into my life as my Savior and Lord,

NOW, THEREFORE:

I do hereby claim, certify, and proclaim that I was Spiritually Born Again through God's Spirit on _____, and I am a Child of God with eternal citizenship in the Kingdom of God.

_____

Signature

ATTENDED
AND ATTESTED
BY: THE HOLY SPIRIT

RECORDED IN THE BOOK
OF LIFE, AND SEALED
BY: JESUS CHRIST

This a representation of the Spiritual Birth recorded in The Lamb's Book of Life in heaven.

MY SPIRITUAL
BIRTHDAY LIST

Name	Date

THE SPIRITUAL BIRTHDAY SONG

Joy - ous day,   Joy - ous day,   When Je - sus washed   your sins a - way!

He's in your heart   to live and stay,   And we re - joice   with you to - day.

Joy - ous day,   Joy - ous day,   It's _Name's_   Spirit - ual Bir - th   Day!

MUSIC: "Happy Day"; Unknown; *ref. attr.* to Edward F. Rimbault, 1854. Public Domain.